Handbook for Commercializing Alien Technology
by Tim Raines

© Timothy Raines, 2024

Editing by
Emilie Clemmens, PhD
and Lauren Udwari

Cover and Interior Design by
Arjan Van Woensel

ISBN: 978-1-965016-19-0

PLATYPUS
PUBLISHING

TABLE OF CONTENTS

ENDORSEMENTS

"This book is a must-read for any technical founder ready to transform a breakthrough innovation into a market-shaping product. The Handbook for Commercializing Alien Technology takes complex ideas and turns them into clear, actionable steps, making the challenging path to commercialization engaging and achievable. With its inventive approach, this guide shows that launching an extraordinary technology can be as exhilarating as it is rewarding. A perfect roadmap for anyone serious about bringing deep tech to the world."

— Dean Becker, ROKiT, Group Vice-Chairman and CEO, Co-Founder Becker Transactions, Founder Ocean Tomo Transactions, and Founder ICAP Patent Brokerage

"The Handbook for Commercializing Alien Technology is a fun and insightful guide for deep tech startups, offering essential strategies to craft compelling pitches, secure investment, and build a foundation for long-term success. Those raising funding will find this insightful and informative."

— Hall Martin, TEN Capital Network, CEO

"Change can feel to some of us like we're moving to another planet. In this fun, engaging book, Timothy Raines unpacks how to bring new technologies down to earth so that innovations prove useful and acceptable. After all, the last thing innovators want to do is create products that alienate people! This fun and inspiring read runs with the 'alien' metaphor, providing insights and tips that help readers appreciate how truly far out some innovations can feel. As a science communicator, I particularly loved the sections that emphasize how important it is to communicate with empathy and clarity, really aiming to understand what people need."

"A concise, accessible, and deeply useful guide for first-time hardtech founders. If you are considering the fraught trip from the lab to a commercial product, start your journey here."

EMILIE –
THANK YOU FOR EDITING &
CONTRIBUTING! I HAVE
ENJOYED WORKING WITH YOU.

Office Memorandum • **UNITED STATES GOVERNMENT**

Office of Technology Transfer
██████████ PhD
Washington, DC

SUBJECT:
Flying Saucers
Antigravity Devices
Quantum ████████████
Unlimited Energy Sources

██████████
██████████
██████████

Dear ██████████ PhD,

Researchers across federal labs, universities, and private corporate
R&D partners have been instructed to disclose and, ultimately,
commercialize **ALIEN** innovations to the benefit of economic and
social well-being.

The majority of these innovations are of **ALIEN** origin and unknown
to the greater market; therefore, the utmost care in market approach
should be utilized. It is imperative that your office encourage
researchers to take appropriate risks and provide them with the
tools they need to launch these innovations successfully.

In the interest of national security, it should be known that
most ALIEN innovations may cause alarm in the marketplace and
face rejection or failure to launch. To avoid this, all research
must be translated into value propositions that resonate with the
appropriate target.
████████████████████████████

We strongly encourage you to instruct researchers to seek private
sector guidance toward successful commercialization to increase the
likelihood of success.

Because of the sensitivity of the innovation source and the
technology-centric orientation of our researchers, your office is
expected to downplay the innovation in favor of market understanding
and impact.

ACTION: Disclose to all researchers a path to successful
commercialization of ██████████████

INTRODUCTION

"Any sufficiently advanced technology
is indistinguishable from magic."
— **Arthur C. Clarke**

Given the technology inflow and outflow I've seen from visits and work with teams from Wright-Patterson AFB, White Sands, Sandia, Los Alamos, Yuma Proving Grounds, DARPA, NASA, USSOCOM, NASA JPL, the International Space Station, and more, I am convinced that most technologies I've seen are alien.

I've used a camera system to see vehicles 50 meters deep in a forest. Alien. A helmet that uses three of the five human senses to help pilots feel, hear, see, and locate objects and their distance anywhere around them. Alien. Brain implants that when powered on, shut off disease symptoms, freeing people to return to some normalcy. Alien. A semiconductor chip connected to (harmlessly harvested) live animal cells that saves humans from chemical attacks—and prevents animals from having to serve as "canaries in coal mines." Alien. Spray-on metallic nanoparticle material applied so thin and light to something soft, such as a plastic straw, that can withstand 100kg of pressure before being crushed. Alien.

Your iPhone. GPS. Golden Rice. Dall-E. All Alien.

After seeing and supporting hundreds of advanced science technologies, I can confidently say that they are all alien—and particularly alien to the marketplace when they were conceived.

Why do some alien technologies make it into our daily lives, while others never make it out of the lab? What separates successful and unsuccessful commercialization comes down to an innovator's

1

willingness to admit that their technology is alien, and then adjust how they think about, act within, and integrate into the market to make it a reality—and benefit society.

Arthur C. Clarke thought of innovative technology as "magic," a concept that is no more outlandish than thinking of such technology as "alien." Only once you realize that the market will see deep tech as alien, can you begin to understand what it will take to succeed in bringing it to market.

Humans may talk big about wanting sci-fi technologies; in reality, bringing anything new to market scares people, and most who try, fail.

Because your target market thinks of new technology as alien your go-to-market strategy must be carefully planned. It must be socialized with the right people first: early adopters. Those people's needs must be carefully dissected before they even get a chance to play with the technology. The greater market must also be explored well before investing in product development. Will they be ready? Are they interested? What design and functional considerations must be taken into account? What problem does it solve and how valuable is the solution? What impact will it have on people and the planet?

Arthur C. Clarke's Complete Three Laws of Innovation

1. When a distinguished but elderly scientist states that something is possible, he is almost certainly right. When he states that something is impossible, he is very probably wrong.
2. The only way of discovering the limits of the possible is to venture a little way past them into the impossible.
3. Any sufficiently advanced technology is indistinguishable from magic.

Tim Raines' Complete Three Laws of Commercialization

1. When an innovator deeply knows the market pain and need from direct insights and can tie their product value proposition to these insights, the path to successful commercialization becomes possible. When innovators believe in their technology with no market validation, they are very probably wrong.

2. The only way to discover an innovation's potential is to deeply explore the customer experience.

3. Any sufficiently advanced technology is alien to the market.

CHAPTER ONE

THE PRIME DIRECTIVE
Are They Ready?

Not all alien technology is suitable for humanity. The most critical thing you can do when evaluating advanced technology–and the first step toward commercializing it–is to determine if the innovation has a benefit and to whom.

We might start by asking, "Is humanity ready for this?" But substitute "humanity" for "the market."

A new technology may have a market but is rarely suitable for all markets. Those rare exceptions are called "exponential technologies"–innovations that can serve more than a billion people. Commercializing these technologies is necessary, and projects like the "X Prize" seek to do just that.

In most cases, you'll need to determine which market will benefit and then obsessively pursue that market. Be warned: it is easy to overestimate the benefit. You've seen behind the curtain and know what the innovation can do because you're close to it. But more often than not, how you think it can help does not align with the market need or interest.

In the fictional universe of Star Trek, the Prime Directive is to not interfere with the normal development of any life or society, even if it is helpful. For our purposes, we'll define Prime Directive a bit differently because it is our civilization and we want to bring new technology into our civilization.

Product/Market Fit

The Prime Directive for commercialization (on this planet, at least) is to determine what marketers call "product/market fit." Innovative technology can only happen by first determining which market has a pain or need that the technology can address. Bridging that gap creates measurable and identifiable value.

The primary consideration is value. At the start of your commercialization venture, you need to determine the value proposition that resonates with your target market. Articulating the value proposition requires creating a short, compelling statement that presents the innovation in a way that creates interest. To generate interest, you must know your audience. Thus, the foundation for creating a meaningful value proposition is understanding the market need by directly interfacing with the people who reflect the market.

When creating your value statement, you naturally begin with what you know about the innovation. These are the "features" (what the technology does) from the perspective of your knowledge and expertise. Features are easy for scientists and engineers to identify and discuss. However, value goes beyond features; you have to relate your innovation to what humans want or need.

Let's consider a recent discovery of a handheld alien ▬▬▬▬▬ ▬▬▬▬▬ technology you have in the lab that allows you to open a wormhole safely and instantly. The primary feature is that you can open a wormhole. Other features include its safety and compactness. Initially, this is a very exciting development, and you may want to get this out to the market quickly. However, this is a dangerous way to approach the market. If you present this technology in a feature-centric way, it likely won't be well received. In fact, you may suddenly and mysteriously disappear, having been hustled to an underground bunker. This would significantly diminish your chances of explaining and bringing the innovation to market. It raises far too many questions, and you are not likely to be taken seriously, hurting your chances to demonstrate the innovation's value. Features are essential, but they aren't everything. The first step is to document the features of the innovation that add to the value proposition.

Discovery

The next piece of the value puzzle to consider is what humans (aka, the market) really want and need related to the innovation. How will they benefit? Examples of market needs related to our wormhole innovation are better understanding our universe and accessing more resources. Put this way, the market can focus on the benefits of opening a wormhole rather than their associated fears or concerns.

It can be helpful to get more granular, especially as you learn more about a particular audience or market to whom you plan to present the innovation. This is called customer discovery, which we'll discuss in depth in chapter two. For now, think of your primary target audience/market and distill the benefits into something that speaks specifically to them. For example, when talking to Amazon, the benefit of accessing any place in the universe through a wormhole is being able to instantly deliver a package from a warehouse in California to a home in Japan.

And here's another example from a technology we use extensively today but was only released for civilian use in 1990: GPS. If you focused on the feature that lets you always know your coordinates, you'd likely fail to impress your audience. But suppose you know a particular business is in ground transportation logistics, explaining that a GPS-enabled map and digital screen could get drivers from point A to point B using the most efficient route possible, saving time and money while increasing revenue with more throughput. In that case, you'd get their attention because you considered the benefit from their unique perspective.

Pains, Gains, and Need

The third step in developing the value proposition is to consider market pain: a problem for which customers feel there is no adequate solution. Market pains are often the most significant motivators for commercialization. For example, a business leader who needs to meet with multiple clients experiences market pain in the form of frustrating airline delays, highway traffic, and pressure to close deals by the end of the fiscal quarter. A portable wormhole generator can also solve this person's pain. Understanding market pain is a critical step in establishing market value. Consider more than pain for a holistic picture, such as needs and gains. Needs may not be as extreme as pains but would convert to demand for your innovation. Gains are the "surprise" factor—for example, an entity multiplying their revenue by using your innovation.

Pulling this together, we can develop a value proposition: a statement that resonates with your target market so you can successfully commercialize your innovation. At this stage, a value proposition helps generate interest while you interview market experts and end-users for deeper discovery and value prop refinement. The value proposition should be iterative and flexible, as what you learn over time will inform a sharper understanding of market pain and corresponding value.

The exercise below will guide you through creating a value proposition for your technology. Consider bringing your team together off-site and using a whiteboard to open up your creativity and collaboratively ideate.

```
ALIEN TIP 001

How to approach the market

DON'T
"We have a new handheld device that allows
anyone to create a wormhole at any time and
any place!"

DO
"Our innovation makes it possible to
instantly deliver anyone or anything to
any point in the world. It will eliminate
all overhead costs associated with air and
ground travel while eliminating greenhouse
gas emissions."
```

Answer these questions to determine how your innovation will impact the market:

- What is the primary purpose of the innovation?
- What are the most important features of the innovation?
- What are the benefits to a user of each of those features?
- What market will most benefit from this technology (e.g., your primary market)?
- What other markets will benefit? (Brainstorm as

many as you can to identify secondary markets.)

- How will each feature benefit your target market? (You may not have these precisely right, so refine over time as you engage and learn from your target market during the customer discovery phase.)
- What pains, needs, and potential gains does your target market have?
- How does your innovation solve your target market's pains and needs, and provide gains?

Now that you've spent some time considering your innovation from your target market's perspective, you are better positioned to determine if the technology should be commercialized. There is a lot more to do in the commercialization process before you can fully determine the technology's viability for the market, but having a solid understanding of the value proposition helps evaluate product/market fit. The next chapter of customer discovery will give us a better understanding of product/market fit.

CHAPTER TWO

I HAVE GOT TO GET ME ONE OF THESE!
Customer Discovery and Product/Market Fit

In the movie *Independence Day*, Captain Steve Hiller (Will Smith) flies an alien ship out of the (not-so-secret) secret DoD base, screaming, "I have got to get me one of these!" You might feel the same enthusiasm for your alien tech, especially since you fully understand and appreciate its capabilities.

The reality, however, is that very few people will react with such positivity to your technology, at least in the early stages. Your passion for your innovation is light years ahead of your potential customers, so you must instead be methodical about how you begin to create interest that matches your own. That starts with connecting with people in the market.

Most innovations will not have the appeal of an intergalactic fighter craft. Nonetheless, other "Captain Hillers" are out there looking for technology like yours. Finding them is critical to commercialization success. You're more likely to find them by understanding who can benefit from the tech and then explaining that benefit in a way that gets them to respond emphatically, "I've got to have one of these!"

Question: Was Captain Hiller "buying" an alien technology or was he "buying" something else?

When you think about product/market fit, the answer to success is that customers do not buy a product, they buy a WIN. This is the essence of product/market fit or making a sale. You are selling a "win" or a "result", which is what the customer wants, not a product. To know what result they want or what a win is to them, ask the market directly.

Unfortunately, for most scientists, engineers, and technologists, the prospect of engaging the market is as daunting as facing a technologically superior alien race that is hell-bent on destroying the planet. Several factors at play create unnecessary fear. From an internal perspective, we do not want to find out our idea has no merit, and we don't want to be so self-assured that we refuse to test that idea and be proven wrong.

From an external perspective, the market is constantly under fire from other life forms (your competitors or alternatives) buzzing around, creating noise and distraction. If innovators are afraid to be told their innovation and their life's work are invalid, and when innovators won't take the time to understand the market pain, they simply become one of many in the vast swarm of pests hoping to get the market's attention.

The key to success is to get deeply invested in the market's perspective. What would they consider to be a "win"? Get out of the lab, garage, or co-working space and discover what the market truly wants and needs. A survey of one doesn't cut it, either. If you're funded through a challenge or grant, go beyond the funded need/topic to find out who else has the problem, a similar problem, or an adjacent problem and see if your innovation has product-market fit there.

As you launch, your "UFO technology" will inevitably encounter a "UMO": Unidentified Market Opportunity. You must rigorously pursue UMOs and uncover their secrets to succeed. Attacking a market is not too different than attacking a planet—the inhabitants have no idea you're there, whatever ideas they might have about you are probably wrong, and unless you discover their perspective, they'll most certainly misinterpret your intentions. Scout before you attack. Live in their skin—figuratively, of course.

There are several ways to assess your target market. One approach may be enough, or a combination of approaches could be required. Generally, using multiple market research methodologies is ideal.

Let's cover the ways to know your market at a high level:

Secondary Research

Secondary research is almost always required and worthwhile. For one, it is relatively easy to do at a high level. Internet searches will often provide the data you need. If you are not funded, you can get two essential data points in almost all cases by a simple search—the size of your potential market and the growth rate (CAGR). The press releases of expensive market reports will tell you these, and often, they will even mention other critical points such as market drivers, competitors, and more.

Buying one of these reports, ranging from $2,500 to 4,500, may be tempting. The full report may break down further niche segments or other data that is more relevant to your needs, but these reports are generally not of value to an early-stage venture. Indeed, if you are applying for grant funding, it is overkill. If you are funded but pre-revenue, it will not likely be a solid investment. Before you buy, be sure you have exhausted all secondary resources and have done some significant primary research, which we will discuss later.

You may discover, however, that you feel you need the nuanced data of these reports, which can include insights on market dynamics such as barriers to entry, drivers that are making it grow or decline—such as environmental, regulatory changes, consumer behavior, or merger and acquisition activity, competitive landscape, and much more. The great news for many of you is that your position in your university as faculty or a student or with a federal lab can often give you access to many of these expensive reports for free. For universities, check with your library for database access; federal labs may have these available through technology transfer or business offices.

Another possible path to get information from these reports without buying is to simply change your search string to see if you can get insights by adding phrases such as "barriers to entry" or "market drivers."

Some additional reconnaissance can help you understand more about the market's pains and needs. If public companies will use the technology you are commercializing, search for their quarterly and annual reports and 10Ks that outline many of their problems and how they think about them. Leveraging financial information can help close a deal later in the commercialization process.

Still, other companies, both large and small, publish a great deal of content on their needs and industry insights through blogs, interviews, industry speaking engagements, podcasts, and more. Other critical secondary research efforts include intellectual property assessments, such as patent and trademark searches, regulatory requirements, competitive assessment, and even searching scientific papers for possible emerging innovations that could impact your success.

Finally, association and industry trade shows are yet another resource for determining interest and need for your innovation. Attending these events can provide a wealth of information on the market and its pain points and help you build a list of future contacts for possible partners and customers.

Attending these conferences can yield valuable intel and push you into human interaction. This is how we move from secondary research to more targeted (and even higher-value) primary research. It is worth pointing out that attendance is much more important than exhibiting at this stage, perhaps any stage. Get out and talk to people, you can meet far more people going to them than hoping they will come to you in a booth you've paid thousands of dollars for.

Primary Research

Primary research comes directly from market sources, such as end-users and experts. There are several ways to conduct this kind of research, each depending on the target market. For example, approach innovation that serves consumers with online surveys of hundreds or thousands of respondents and more in-depth direct interviews. For business-to-business (B2B) solutions, direct interviews alone will likely be sufficient to uncover the opportunity.

For innovators with little or no experience engaging the market or are nervous about engaging in marketing and sales activity, experts are an excellent starting place to get you engaged and overcome any fears of talking to the market. An upside is that they may give you referrals to end-users, making engaging with the market less daunting.

Experts know the industry very well but will not be users of your technology. These are excellent resources and a comfortable place to start the primary research. It is often easier to approach these experts versus end-users because a) you are not likely to appear like you are selling something, b) they generally enjoy talking about the industry, and c) they get paid and become more effective in their jobs when they know what innovations are emerging.

Experts can be university faculty, trade association executives, non-profit executives, industry journalists, or even bloggers with large followings and a pulse of industry happenings. Often, experts will refer you to end-users or, in the case of association executives, even mass-mail your requests for interviews to their members.

Keep in mind that experts do not substitute for end-user contact. Experts do not have the problems an end-user will have; they do not have to decide whether your value justifies parting with a cash investment, and no expert call will result in a future sale. Ultimately, you must make contact with end-users.

End-user interviews are the most important part of primary interviews. Until you speak to people who might buy the solution, you will not know if your innovation can solve their problem. Speaking to end-users can be daunting, especially for innovators who have spent most of their education and career in the lab. Unfortunately, success demands that they be engaged.

Here are some helpful things to consider:

- End-users are generally peers interested in the same things you are. You likely know many of them from industry events. Avoid approaching them as if you're selling something so they're more receptive to talking.
- If you are grant-funded by one of the national labs, the DoD, or a university, consider saying something like, "I am researching an innovation funded by X institution, and we would appreciate your insights on..." If you are truthful about the situation, being affiliated with a larger institution can help lower their guard.
- Never approach someone with an intent to sell. This should be fine, as alien technology is still in development at this stage. When doing customer discovery, focus on discovery and a genuine desire to understand end-user problems. As is often the case, an end-user may ask to be contacted again as the innovation takes shape. If that happens, simply take a note and follow up when appropriate. These contacts are your "early adopters" and often will be happy to buy and provide feedback on your product at beta and not care about details like design or buggy features. Their feedback at this stage is more valuable than a sale and supports you in putting your best product out there when the time is right.

Another great approach to primary research for larger niche markets is to leverage online survey tools. Online surveys allow you to collect a more extensive data set, which gives you added confidence in your primary research. It is important to remember that customer interviews are required; surveys are the only tool for expanding reach and building a more reliable dataset. Getting emails for larger groups can be difficult, but they can sometimes be purchased or leveraged through industry/trade associations. You can also get large lists of targets from attending trade shows, which often will provide a spreadsheet of all exhibitors and attendees.

Apply your scientific rigor to understanding UMOs, and your chances of success will significantly increase. Dig deep to uncover the market's needs and problems, and be honest with yourself about your tech's ability to meet a market need. Also, do not fall in love with your initial idea. Be open to the possibility that you're wrong and use the information you uncover to adjust or even pivot your business model entirely. As a founder, take ownership of this understanding and build relationships such that you are responsible for the outcome.

The MVP

No matter how much information you gather on the market through secondary and primary research, proper Customer Discovery isn't complete until the technology is tested. Historically, alien experimentation on humans has been frowned upon. Certainly, abductions are out of the question. So, how do you proceed to see how humans respond to the innovation?

It is critical to get the technology in the hands of your target market and measure the results. Do not keep the innovation in the lab until it meets your final vision. Test prototypes as early as possible with people you have identified as early adopters and gather feedback to take them back to the lab and iterate further. Your prototype is called the "minimally viable product" or MVP.

MVPs often are quite simple and creative, maybe even a sticky note for a possible button location. Just like Captain Hiller's "forward, reverse" paper taped to the console, it can be easily flipped over by the user and that data could change how you thought users might engage with the product.

The first MVP should be just a core piece of the technology or a mock-up that functions well enough to gauge interest. It is important to seek out early adopters who will not care how well the technology is designed, whether it solves all of their problems or is even a bit buggy. Early adopters are the kinds of people who are anxious to know what alien technology might be like and what it might do. Seek them out and get feedback on what works, what doesn't, what is interesting, and other insights. With that information, return to the lab, iterate, and test again. Return to the early adopters, measure, and iterate until you know it will be well received.

Engaging the market in this way is a part of the Lean Startup methodology popularized by Eric Ries. When you proceed this way, you improve the chances of success at a much lower cost and refrain from unleashing something the world is not ready to accept.

CHAPTER THREE

"If we have all of this amazing
innovation, then where are the deals?"
— **Tim Raines**

SHAPESHIFTING
Becoming an Entrepreneur

I call this the Alien Tech Paradox—apologies to Enrico Fermi. There is a lot of great innovation out there. In the commercialization process, the volume of barriers can be overwhelming. However, in most cases, the biggest blocker of successful commercialization is whether or not the team leading the effort can go the distance.

The questions to ask yourself are:
- Are you the right person to do this?
- Do you want to do this?
- Can you shapeshift into a startup leader?

The greatest skill you can learn from aliens is shapeshifting. To bring a new technology to market, you'll have to stretch yourself to fit in—and excel at—uncomfortable situations.

Some shapeshifters are excellent; some aren't. In *Star Trek*,

Changlings like Odo, are savvy shapeshifters, perfectly embodying the human form, working hard to assimilate by learning the culture, behaviors, and ways of thinking. Alternatively, Edgar the Bug from *Men in Black* barely shrinks himself into a human skin with cringy and comical results. Are you truly committed to being a successful shapeshifter? Are you Odo or Edgar the Bug?

Be honest with yourself.

When you have spent your entire education and career devoted to your science and research, it can be difficult and uncomfortable to do what it takes to bring a technology to market. Generally speaking, you have three choices:

- Launch and lead your startup
- Cultivate a partnership to license your technology
- Turn over your IP to your institution to market on your behalf

No choice is easy and all have trade-offs. Each choice but one requires you to leave your research behind and shapeshift, most likely for a longer period than anticipated, if not forever. Are you prepared to make this commitment?

Who Are You?

*"A journey of a thousand miles
begins with a single step."*
– Lao Tzu (attributed)

The first step in deciding to lead your innovation to market is to come to grips with who you are and what you are willing to do to achieve your goal. Understanding your options and various paths to commercialization will help you to align what you are willing to do with what and how it must be done.

The great news is that current entrepreneurial theory suggests that *anyone* can be a successful entrepreneur. There is no fixed persona, no requirement to be extroverted, a risk taker, or any other fixed characteristics. What's required is being truthful to yourself as to whether or not you *want* to put in the effort to lead a successful startup–this requires A LOT OF EFFORT.

Research or Die

If you truly want to make your technology a reality, then you'll have to leave your lab. If you only want to be a researcher and be in the lab every day working on your ideas, then you are not likely to succeed and there is a very slim chance the innovation will materialize.

This path is not uncommon. You know yourself, including the fact that you would not enjoy the commercialization journey. In this case, all you have to do is disclose your IP to your technology transfer office (TTO) and they will do all of the work. With all due respect to Tech Transfer professionals, let's be frank–their shapeshifting skills are about as evolved as Edgar the Bug. If you can walk away from the technology you have invested in and have no expectations that it will ever see the light of day, this might be your best choice.

Numerous studies show that most TTOs operate at a loss to the university–even fewer generate significant income from technology licensing. To be fair, commercialization is very difficult. Startups have low success rates too, but you can greatly increase your odds of success when you take control. You are invested in the idea, no one else. If possible, take the lead. If not, handing over control is your best option–a valid choice.

License your IP

Licensing or selling your IP is the middle ground. Your TTO will do this, with no need for you to participate. However, if you are dedicated to seeing the alien tech in the hands of humans, then you should create a startup and license the IP yourself from your institution.

When you take this route, you can raise capital to advance the technology and increase earnings for your efforts. This capital can be non-diluted, usually from government institutions.

During this process, you still can go all in to take the tech to market, raise venture capital, hire people, and build and scale a real company. Alternatively, as you develop the tech further, you can make relationships with larger companies that you intend to license the IP to as go-to-market (GTM) partners. In this scenario, you will still likely profit more from royalties than going with your TTO and can return to your lab or next innovation relatively soon.

The upside is that your TTO will often assist to some level. You can also hire outside resources with deep experience in licensing deals and more connections with the technology scouts of larger target companies.

You will also want to network and access technology scouts at these target companies, which later chapters will cover.

Full Startup Mode

Becoming a viable startup that realizes real value means shapeshifting from scientist to business-minded CEO. If you envision building not just a technology, but a company that creates jobs, generates millions or billions of dollars in revenue, and can be sold to another company or IPO, then you're on a path of serious commitment. You may never see a lab or tinker with the technology again (or at least not for many years).

As a startup CEO, you'll learn new skills, focus on relationship building, learn to sell and raise capital, and more. It is often said, "The founder makes this first sale," and this is true. As CEO, you will be selling from the beginning of the commercialization process, all the way to your first dollar of revenue. Even if you plan to sell your idea to a VC and hire sales, you'll find that most of the time investment will not come until you've sold something already.

If being the CEO does not sound right for you, but you are passionate about taking ownership of your technology's success, there are options. This path can still be viable if you have the right co-founder or equity partner. In an ideal world, you'll go on the commercialization journey with a partner invested in your success. If there's someone you trust with the skills and experience to lead the business while you lead product development, then this is perfectly acceptable—you can be co-founder and CTO. This person must be equally invested in the business, in both interest in and understanding of the innovation and market and equity in the company. They must have shared risk and reward.

You may have begun alone or with a core group of technologist peers. In this case, you can still choose the startup path and remain CTO, but you should find a qualified CEO and compensate them with significant ownership of the company. It is a bigger risk to bring in someone you don't know well. A good CEO must be properly incentivized—this means giving them significant equity in the company. If you plan to raise investment capital, even the VCs will look at the cap table and leadership; If they do not see the core leadership team properly incentivized, your company may not be investable.

The Final Frontier

If you choose to be a startup entrepreneur, consider it your final frontier. Honestly assess who you are and what you want to do as it relates to your innovation. Anyone can be an entrepreneur, but few people understand what it means to be an entrepreneur or are willing to do what it takes to succeed.

Interview peers who have done this before. Ask them about their experiences and what worked for them and what did not. Ask what they would do differently or what they should warn you about given what they know about you.

If you are committed to the journey, then prepare to shapeshift. The remaining chapters will guide you, but the first and perhaps most important step is learning to communicate.

```
Alien Tip 003

Master the art of shapeshifting like an Odo,
not an Edgar.

Remember
Blending in with the business world doesn't
mean wearing an ill-fitting human suit—
it means truly adapting your skills and
mindset to navigate the strange new world of
entrepreneurship.
```

CHAPTER FOUR

ALIEN TO HUMAN TELEPATHY
the Art of Communication

Anecdotal reports of alien encounters indicate that communication occurs telepathically. As scientists, you'll likely rule out this mode of communication before you've finished reading this sentence. So, the question is, why do you communicate to the market like a scientist? This approach is no more realistic than telepathy.

Communicating advanced technology to the market requires that you speak their language and limit complex language that describes the innovation in all its alien-scientific glory. The market thinks in terms of needs and problems that are relevant to them. If your alien technology is highly complex and/or disruptive, how likely are humans to grasp how it might solve their problems and improve their future?

Discussing only the specific features of the innovation and how groundbreaking you think it is, is to communicate in alien terms. The market responds to benefits, not features. The market responds to solutions that solve specific problems that it has. It does not respond to technical data—it responds to financial impact data that results from solving an unmet need.

Listen, Then Communicate

Psychologists, success experts, and relationship experts all agree that being a listener is the foundation for good communication. "Seek first to understand, then be understood", as Steven Covey famously wrote in his Seven Habits. Even in the search for aliens, we may have ideas about communication we would need to send a signal but The SETI(Search for Extraterrestrial Intelligence) Institute, has, "...to understand..." as the core of its mission statement.

When you engage the market, you must be a listener. When you hire experts, advisors, and consultants for advice outside your skillset, listen to them. You may have all the answers about your innovation but you do not have all of the answers to commercialization and the market. Be open-minded and listen. Be prepared to have your mind changed and admit you could be wrong. Being "wrong" does not mean you cannot succeed with your innovation and startup, you will just learn how to "iterate" or "pivot", to keep going.

Breaking the Code

In 1966, former U.S. Army codebreaker Lambros D. Callimahos wrote a paper outlining possible methods of communication with alien civilizations. The NSA declassified the document "Communication with Extraterrestrial Intelligence" in 2004, and it's available at NSA. gov. The paper posits that math and various cryptography methods would be the most likely way an intelligent civilization could determine signals from another intelligent civilization.

When NASA launched the Voyager spacecrafts, scientists included a golden record with scientific illustrations that could be decoded to explain how to play the record, where Earth can be found, and a method to determine when the spacecraft departed. These forms of communication may be ideal for human-to-alien communication, but when your target market consists of other humans, communicating

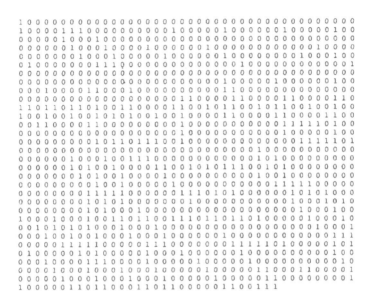

in any form of scientific or technical jargon is a lousy way to persuade them to act. However, the lesson is still the same. Think about how your audience perceives and responds to information.

When commercializing alien technology, you, as a scientist and technologist, sit somewhere between the alien world and the market. In most cases, much closer to alien, to be frank. Just as we need cryptography to communicate with alien intelligence, we should also translate what we have to say to market intelligence.

While we know nothing of value about alien intelligence, we know a lot about human intelligence. Human intelligence in both the scientific and market communities is heavily influenced by emotional intelligence. In other words, communication for commercialization must appeal to the emotional intelligence of the target. It must also deal in logic the market will understand, like financial Return on Investment (ROI) or reduction in carbon emissions, for example.

Buying decisions are complex, so balance your communications using logical and emotional components. The combination of these factors is called value.

The Value Proposition

Once we have exposed the UMO (unidentified market opportunity) through customer discovery, we can develop a communications strategy appropriate for the identified market. The simplest place to start is to develop a value proposition. The value proposition is a simple and short way to communicate what value you plan to deliver to the market that creates interest and deeper engagement. A strong value prop should resonate with your target market by centering on the unmet need you've discovered. And it should be decidedly non-technical.

There are many resources for quickly understanding how to craft a compelling value prop statement. Spend quality time out of the lab with your trusted advisors and co-founders to brainstorm an inspired statement. One of the best places to begin is to use the "Value Proposition Canvas," published by Strategyzer—the foundational work for your statement. It's designed to gain customer and market perspective of their pains, gains, and jobs to be done, which clarifies what they care about and value most.

Once you've developed a value proposition, it will inform your entire marketing strategy and brand. Your value proposition helps keep market-facing materials, like pitch decks and your website, simple and compelling. Even when crafting more technology-oriented materials such as a whitepaper or quad chart, think value first (not technology first), and your marketing content will be more accessible and engaging.

How to Be a Jedi Master Communicator

"These are not the droids we're looking for."
— Easily Influenced Imperial Stormtrooper

The goal of good communication is to be as influential as a Jedi Master. To be a master communicator is to put your target audience at the center of everything you do to communicate, whether written or verbal. This is all based on listening and understanding, without bias towards your technology and what you *think* is right. You only have assumptions and you need to verify your assumptions before you can fully understand.

When you create a pitch deck for investment, sales presentation, or web page, cover the problem or unmet need you intend to solve first, then present your unique solution that aligns with the problem to be solved. The initial solution is not a deep dive into the technology– it's a simple statement of how the innovation solves the problem. Discussion about the workings of the innovation comes after you've captured attention and gained credibility. Credibility with the market means that you have communicated on their terms and are as knowledgeable about their needs as they are, with the added value of a solution.

Verbal communication follows the same principles. When talking to someone, we respond more positively to people who listen, express genuine interest, and don't dominate the entire conversation. Approaching the market is no different than basic conversational etiquette.

When you speak to a possible investor, partner, or customer, avoid launching into the details that excite you about the technology. Talk to them about their business, ask them about their challenges, and find out how they've approached possible solutions. Begin by building rapport with your audience. When you have built trust, you can begin to engage in discussion around your innovation. When you do discuss the technology, speak in high-level terms about your value proposition and what you've discovered about a possible path to a solution, and try to keep the dialogue balanced throughout. Let them ask questions and continue to learn.

When you communicate appropriately, you'll feel telepathic. You start getting the responses you want and access to the information you need. Remember, when selling alien technology, everything you know about it is complex cryptography to others. The market is not interested in spending time cracking the code; they want simple, direct communication that demonstrates you understand the problem and have a compelling solution that adds value.

Alien Tip 004

Embrace the great Richard Feynman's four step "Feynman Technique", especially step 2, which is to be able to break down your complex concept into something you can teach to a child.

CHAPTER FIVE

CROP CIRCLES, PYRAMIDS, AND ASTROLOGICAL MONUMENTS
The Importance of Branding

Crop circles, Stonehenge, the Great Pyramids–many ancient artifacts defy easy explanation. Whether human-made or extraterrestrial, these artifacts engage our imagination. They challenge us to consider culture, purpose, and capacities beyond our current perspectives as we seek to understand the technology behind them and how they may have served ancient communities.

These icons are important in the same way your new venture's brand will be important.

A brand is more than a logo; it represents your core principles. It orients your audience to the experience they will have by engaging with you. Build your brand on key pillars, including purpose, perception, identity, values, and expertise.

Brand Pyramid

While science has debunked the Pyramid of Giza's alignment with Orion, and no treasure was found or documented, we still associate the Pyramid with the pharaoh's treasures. Your brand is your treasure. It is the sum of your assets. It represents the product and services you deliver, the mission and vision behind your reason for existing, and the market's perception of who you are, what you do, and, most importantly, why you do what you do.

Brand Observatory

Ancient observatories, such as Stonehenge, Chichen Itza, Newgrange, Machu Picchu, or the Beijing Ancient Observatory, guided seasonal change and connected our earthly experience with the universe by understanding the movements of the stars, helping humans see the "bigger picture." Your brand is how you are perceived. It is the bigger picture for your customers and the market. It is critical to think beyond the innovation itself, beyond revenues, beyond growth, and consider how your new venture fits into the bigger picture and the positive impact it will represent.

Brand Crop Circles

The more temporary counterparts to the archaeo-astronomical structures, crop circles are frequent and fresh. Once you have established your brand strategy, aligning your messaging through all marketing communications and customer engagements is critical to remaining relevant. Your brand is a living, breathing phenomenon grounded in core principles. Create cohesiveness in how you, your employees, your product, and your marketing efforts represent your brand.

Many technology entrepreneurs view concepts such as branding, marketing, and product positioning with about as much skepticism as they hold toward an alien origin for ancient artifacts. Ignoring the power of branding, however, is a mistake. While some mysteries may yet surround the construction of these landmarks, few mysteries remain regarding the impact that branding can have on venture success. We have mountains of data supporting the power of branding and its role in aligning your commercialization goals with the market's interests.

To develop an engaging brand, you must consider your company from the inside out. Your brand comprises two major components: the soul and spirit of your brand that comes from your purpose and the external execution of the brand promise through visual and written communication.

Soul and Spirit: Who and Why

The soul and spirit of your company are who you are and why you are bringing innovation to the market–this is often called the "brand promise" and informs what the market will expect each time they engage with your company. Many techniques have been developed to consider this aspect of brand development. You are likely aware of "mission" and "vision" and perhaps have already written up these classic business tools for your startup. You may also know newer philosophies like Simon Sinek's "Golden Circle." There are dozens of resources for digging into this aspect of brand development, and you should dedicate time to consider how you want to be perceived.

There is no one toolset or branding thought leadership that will guarantee your success. Thought leaders constantly launch new and innovative ideas in this area, so use what resonates with you. You'll find that one of these tools–or a combination of tools–is the best approach to building your brand foundation.

The most important thing required for branding success is authenticity in your passion for helping the world. Having positive intentions to create value is the starting place for success. When you genuinely desire to add value—and hire others who get behind your reason for bringing your innovation to market—you are well-positioned to succeed in cultivating a positive reception from customers.

ALIEN TIP 005

Be able to answer these questions about your brand
- What is your venture's purpose?
- What characteristics define your brand?
- How do you want to be perceived in the marketplace?

Brand Visuals and Content

When it comes to branding, most humans think of the visual aspects alone. While the visual elements of a brand are important, so is the content. One of the most common mistakes scientists and engineers make when bringing alien tech to market is failing to ensure consistency in visual and written brand elements.

Just because you can code and develop a website and use online design tools does not mean you should! While we strongly encourage minimally viable products (MVPs) and testing your business model in the market, your web presence is not an expensive investment—and it's the first place people will go to get a sense of who you are and what you are about.

A good designer will work with you to develop a logo and website that reflects your core brand promise and principles. Your designer should also develop a style guide that will inform future marketing materials to ensure consistency. It's also a good idea to have them design a pitch deck since this is one of the first things people will see when you start socializing your alien tech to the world. The style guide includes colors, fonts, and other key items that keep your brand visuals consistent across the internet, pitch decks, presentations, and all other marketing materials.

Content consistency is also critical—another area where scientists and engineers tend to think from the alien tech perspective rather than the human and market perspective. Good content is developed from the market's perspective. Demonstrate that you understand the market need and problem, then outline your solution in a value-based rather than a technology—and feature-based way.

Most scientists and technologists bringing alien tech to market tend to be overly excited about the innovation's technical merits. As a result, the website's content and pitch decks are full of complex alien-speak that the market will likely reject. Your innovation is new, so written content and illustrations should be simple and focus on the potential to solve big problems. Do this before diving deeper with your audience and getting into the how. You'll enter the deal-making process as a trusted ally if done correctly.

A brand at its best is an external influence that aligns with the stories its target market cares most about—their own stories.

Remain relevant through frequent engagement. Create content relevant to your expertise that drives interest and curiosity in the innovation. Create content that makes early adopters feel like they've discovered you, not that they've been sold. Humans are discoverers. If alien tech was dropped right before them, it might scare them.

But if they feel like they've discovered something no one else knows about, they'll be your champion and spread the word to other buyers.

Create human discoverers with content that is interesting, informative, and adds value to their story. Write content that gives them insights—via blogs, journals, or carefully structured advertising. No matter how you reach your audience, maintain brand authenticity—and consistency!

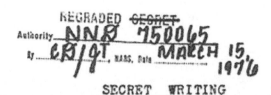

CHAPTER SIX

WE COME IN PEACE
Innovate for Good

Another famous maxim among aliens is, "We come in peace." Their alien technology, though, could improve or destroy the planet! You'll need to reassure others that yours will do no harm. As you approach the humans (the market) with your alien tech, it is critical to "commercialize in peace."

Of course, technology (alien or otherwise) often can help and harm. Nuclear technology can destroy or create near-limitless clean energy. Artificial intelligence can relieve humans from mundane tasks, or it might subvert critical life support systems and infrastructure and generate dangerous disinformation.

In the September 1965 issue of "Soviet Life," renowned astronomer and astrophysicist Professor Iosif Shklovsky outlined the five reasons a civilization that was sufficiently advanced beyond ours at that time might have already destroyed itself:

1. Self-destruction as a result of a thermonuclear catastrophe or some other discovery that may have unpredictable and uncontrollable consequences.
2. Genetic danger.
3. Overproduction of information.
4. Restricted capacity of the individual's brain, which can lead to excessive specialization, with consequent dangers of degeneration.
5. A crisis precipitated by the creation of artificially intelligent beings.

Today, all five are realistic concerns. AI, information sciences, and biotechnology innovators are closest to determining whether these technologies serve or destroy humanity. Nuclear weapons or nuclear medicine and clean, reliable energy? Gene editing for longevity or eugenics? Information to learn or information to deceive? AI to allow humans to focus on innovation and creativity or to master our systems and institutions?

When you bring an alien innovation to the market, come in peace.

Grey Area

The reality is that most innovation, just like most things in life, are not black and white. Most innovations initially succeed on a primary benefit but come at a cost in other ways. So what do we do then?

A great example of this would be electric vehicles, or EV's. EV's have been successful because battery innovation is able to deliver driving ranges that are comparable to combustion vehicles. Adoption was fast because once this hurtle was overcome, an EV, when compared to a combustion vehicle, is blindingly fast, has no torque curve, quiet, no emissions, and initially less expensive to power. EV's, however, had a bit of an issue when it came to delivering on the question of, "is this innovation good for the people and planet?" The issue is that batteries require the mining of rare earth minerals, are difficult to dispose of or recycle, and are arguably no better for the environment than their combustion counterparts, just in different ways.

The answer to this question is not easy but generally speaking, moving forward to make a positive impact in one way, is the right thing to do, even if other issues crop up. Humans tend to do the right thing and innovation is in our blood, so while EV's might cause some issues with mining and battery development, it has spurred a lot of new innovation in discovering alternatives to rare earth metals, innovation in battery design, recycling, and materials, an innovation in competitive industries, including combustion engines that might not have occurred had they not been challenged by a new rival technology.

We cannot always anticipate how an alien technology will impact the earth in the short and long term but we can be aware that there *will* be an impact and do what we can to minimize negative impact and move forward ethically.

The key is to have the right perspective.

The "Triple Bottom Line"

Great corporations have adopted the triple bottom line rule, a concept credited to sustainable business author and serial entrepreneur John Elkington. Rather than focusing solely on personal success, the triple bottom line rule suggests that innovators focus on three Ps: people, the planet, and profit. Consider how your innovation and company mission impact each of these areas.

1. People

Hire good people and work with good partners. Treat them—and your customers—with respect. Bring people into your venture who are motivated by your mission and vision and want to make a positive difference.

2. Planet

Just because your technology is clean-energy or removes space debris doesn't mean you can check off this box. Taking responsibility for planetary health means considering the impacts of every aspect of your business. Reuse and recycle within your buildings, select LEED-certified buildings to rent, or hire a LEED architect if you're fortunate enough to build your offices.

Reward employees for using public transit or commuting by bike. Most importantly, innovate with the planet in mind. Include planetary health as a key factor in your design process. Making changes to protect our planet can seem difficult or inconvenient. Still, by prioritizing planetary health, you can create a positive impact and position your organization for a prosperous future.

3. Profits

Profit is not a dirty word, but do not subjugate anything important to maximizing profits for shareholders. Emphasize your commitment to people and the planet, and use profits to continue innovating, benefit all stakeholders, and remain on task for constant improvement. Play the long game; don't get pressured into short-term greed.

Bring innovations into the world that create prosperity for the whole. Make a positive impact the top priority. As more companies focus on doing good, corporate culture will shift, the three Ps will become the standard, and collective efforts will improve the world.

Focus on alien technology that makes a positive impact on our world. Incorporate positivity into your culture and work environment as well. Keep the planet in mind, and share the profits wisely.

Alien Tip 006

When bringing your alien tech to Earth,
remember: a death ray might impress the
locals, but a clean energy source will win
their hearts.

Always ask yourself: "Would E.T. phone home
about this, or try to conquer it?" Aim for
the former, not the latter.

CHAPTER SEVEN

*"Victorious warriors win first and then
go to war, while defeated warriors
go to war first and then seek to win."*

— **Sun Tzu**

WAR OF THE WORLDS
Competition

Despite the vastness of the universe, you will face competition that hinders your innovation's success. So, the path to winning is first to know your competition. This is not so straightforward, especially with disruptive technologies.

When researchers plan to commercialize alien technologies, one of the most commonly heard phrases is, "We don't have any competition; this is completely new!"

It is critical to realize the difference between traditional competition, where you plan to take market share from existing providers, and other types of competition that often win the battle because they are overlooked:

Alternatives

Alternatives are a commonly overlooked source of competition. They are competitors that present unique ways to get the same job done.

For example, you may have developed a business model that reduces the cost of transporting valuable metals to the emerging low-earth orbit manufacturing industry. Your direct competition might be existing commercial space companies. Your alternative competition would be an asteroid or moon mining company that can deliver the same materials without the costly fuel to leave Earth's orbit.

Current Way of Doing Business

Inertia can be challenging to overcome. Even if there is no direct technology or process competition, you must compete against current processes and systems deemed "good enough" by the market. Change is a perceived risk, and people and bureaucracies have a difficult time accepting change. Proper customer discovery should identify the pain in the current system and create demand for change once you've tied your solution to the identified problem. Still, you'll compete with stakeholders stuck in the current way of doing business and their support systems.

Emerging Innovations and Business Models

For advanced science and technology startups, other labs are one of the most overlooked areas of competition. Ironically, some of the same funding sources that helped you with your R&D are funding competing ideas that may disrupt your business model. Searching scientific papers, university research, and patent databases can often surface competing ideas you must consider. The pace of innovation today is far too quick to ignore new entrants, even when you think your innovation is the one to shake up the industry.

Power Players

Once you progress with the market, be wary of the significant corporate R&D giants. What might not have been on their radar can often become a core business line within months with the money, bright minds, and legal maneuvering that these corporate behemoths can bring to the table. Many times, whether approached for partnerships, licensing, or other means of discovering what you are up to, these companies have built their answer to the problem and are more than capable of squashing your startup. Keep in mind that you are competing for someone's funding and attention, which can be distracted by these competitors or even by inaction or indifference on the part of the market.

When I worked for a major enterprise software company, I made significant inroads with a Fortune 50 computer company. I had an internal champion, networked positively across the matrix of departments, leaders, and users, and had senior executive access. There was a clear "pain" with the existing product and competitor, and millions were budgeted to address the issue. It was a perfect scenario. With the blessing of my management, this deal became my sole customer.

We were confident. We spent two years demonstrating our solution, and the response was overwhelmingly positive. Towards the end of the effort, an executive of the incumbent called me to meet for lunch. They said they were letting go of the client executive and would hire me for twice my current pay plus a higher-than-normal commission to close the deal. At about the same time, my internal champion shared a rough draft of an internal technical decision matrix on which they would base their decision, and we looked solid.

I was so sure of the win that I declined the amazing job offer and prepped for the kill. Within a month, we lost to the incumbent. I lost more than a million dollars in commission and, ultimately, the favor of my management some years later.

The most difficult pill to swallow was that we *had* won—technically. My internal champion shared the final decision matrix, which comprised twelve complex technical decision points, and we won 11 of them by a large margin. The only one we lost was not technical— or rational. It simply read, "incumbent." A Fortune 50 company narrowed down a multi-million-dollar enterprise decision to three competitors. The company thoroughly evaluated these competitors as to which was best for transforming their business, and the decision came down to fear of change and disruption.

While we were not a disruptor and all players were direct competitors, including the incumbent, this is an example of how competition can take on many forms. Even if you are the only game in town, you can lose to the current way of doing business.

Emerging innovation played a role in a failed startup I was a part of in grad school. The concept was genuinely innovative, with no direct competition. We aimed to develop a sensor for indoor and outdoor home gardening to help gardeners select ideal planting locations and actively measure light, soil content, and water to manage plant health. We set about filing provisional patents, developing the prototype, and raising capital.

Within weeks of filing two provisional patents, a major tech publication wrote about two engineers launching a company that set out to do the same thing. It was as if the magazine had written about us—the business model, the product, and the pace of startup activity were the same. The article included a fancy product design image and mentioned patents being filed. We quickly found a patent, and they were nearly identical.

We had done a patent search initially, but this was an example of how fast innovation can move. Our competition could move faster because they were self-funded, and we could not keep pace without closing a seed round, so we decided to fold it and move on. As it turns out, the market didn't want this innovation, and they folded as soon as the product hit the shelf. This experience taught me a valuable lesson: even without direct competition, someone is always working to solve the same problem.

An adage in the venture capital community says, "If you think you have a truly unique idea, you can bet there are at least twenty others in the world with the same idea as yours at this very moment." Their point is that it is all about execution, and they are right. You must execute, but you must also be aware there are others out there, so turn over every rock in the process and never say, "We have no competition."

Alien Tip 007

Just because your spaceship is the only one in the sky doesn't mean you've won the invasion.

In the great radio show and movie, *"War of the Worlds"*, the invaders focused upon and conquered all competitive defenses but they failed to consider a simple virus that led to defeat.

ACT G-51.....

INFO G-5Ø.....G-2Ø......FOLDERS.......

CHAPTER EIGHT

*"For my ally is the Force,
and a powerful ally it is."*
— **Yoda**

USE THE FORCE
Intellectual Property

Protecting an innovation can be the greatest "Force" you can hold and the most critical to success. Without proper protection, you will face more significant challenges from competitors and eliminate your runway to develop a stronghold in the market.

Intellectual property (IP) protection is essential to controlling your outcome regardless of your business model. If you plan to license a technology, IP will protect you as you enter discussions with possible partners who, in most cases, can develop a similar innovation given enough insight. If your business plan is to enter the market yourself, a great IP strategy can help you defend against new entrants long enough to establish your business and control the market.

IP strategy is more than just patents. Other forms of potentially relevant IP include copyright, trademark, and trade secret designations. Each serves a specific purpose, and a good strategy will involve a mix of IP choices that depend on your innovation, business model, and goals.

While there are some stories of innovators who go it alone, few will master "The Force" without a proper Jedi Master—an IP attorney. Suppose you developed your innovation through your work at a national lab or university. In that case, you will have resources to support you in determining your IP strategy and executing the proper processes to secure your innovation. If you do not have these resources, finding an experienced IP attorney familiar with your technology universe is critical. Not all IP attorneys are the same; finding the right fit takes effort.

Attorneys are expensive but worth the investment. With a little effort, it is not uncommon to find an entrepreneurial IP attorney who might be interested in equity and the long-term prospects of your startup. This support is easier to find by joining an accelerator or incubator, a subject for the next chapter.

But before we engage an IP attorney, it is important to understand the basics, be capable of searching for existing IP that might limit your "Freedom to Operate," and know the general use cases for each type of IP protection.

IP Landscape and Freedom to Operate

If your innovation is a physical device, patents are generally the best way to protect it. Before you invest time and money into the R&D, prototyping, and hiring attorneys, you should take some time to investigate whether or not you have the "Freedom to Operate."

Freedom to Operate means that the innovation you plan to patent does not infringe on existing patents. Sources for searching for similar innovations include the US Patent and Trademark Office (USPTO), Google Patents, and the International Patent Documentation Center (INPADOC). Searches should be creative, using several search strings that involve the core subjects that make up your innovation. The results of these searches are also helpful in uncovering competitors and competing methods. Doing patent searches is a valuable way to understand the market and invest your time and money most wisely.

Which Light Saber is Right for You?

A Jedi is most powerful with the right tools, and there are several strategies for protecting your IP. The factors for deciding which to use are determined predominately by the innovation and your business model.

For example, you wouldn't typically seek a patent if you have a software product. Software and algorithms are ideal for leveraging trade secrets and copyrights. These are inexpensive routes to IP protection, the only cost associated with copyright filing. A trade secret is the most robust protection because it can't be reverse-engineered or leaked as long as it remains secret.

Patents are ideal for physical sciences or even pharmaceutical formulations. A patent is a detailed explanation of what you are protecting, alerting others that if they intend to solve the same market problems, they cannot do it the same way, but they require divulging IP to secure the patent.

Your business model also impacts how you approach IP protection. For example, if you expect to remain in the lab, spend time in R&D, and have no interest in running a startup, your business model would likely be to license your innovation. To secure a licensing deal, you'll need to approach more prominent companies that will manufacture and sell the innovation. In these cases, patents are better designed to protect you, as you will need to communicate the innovation in detail through knowledge transfer.

To help you choose your saber (i.e., tool for IP protection), let's discuss each tool in more depth:

Patents

Patents explain your innovation and claims about its function. They are legal documents filed with public entities like the US Government or other foreign governments that help approve the validity and serve as an impartial judicial body should an offense against a patent occur.

Patents are complex, and while many innovators write and file their patents, it is generally best to have a professional IP attorney write and file the patent for the best protection possible. This process is expensive and time-consuming but worth it because it gives you the ability and time to launch a venture and capitalize on the expense of R&D, patenting, and startup costs. It also helps if you license the idea to a company.

Patents, by nature, expose how your innovation works, so it is possible that others can learn from that and engineer around it, or other companies in foreign countries can simply steal your idea and sell it around the globe with little or no recourse to stop it. There is a further expense in filing a patent internationally, but some countries will not recognize your patent, which may or may not present a problem.

Patents are also limited in their lifespan. Generally, there is plenty of time to make the most of a successful patent, but eventually, the patent expires, and your company may face new entrants competing with you at that time. If you have established your market share by then, expiration is less of a concern.

Finally, patents are costly to defend and maintain. After you spend tens of thousands of dollars securing a patent, you must continue to pay to keep it and be constantly vigilant in its defense. Legal fees for patent protection can be extensive. Though those costs may be worthwhile for settlements and judgments against defenders, you will likely spend a lot on attorney fees to stop an infringement with no financial payback.

Trade Secret

A trade secret conceals the "how" and "what" of your innovation. There are many famous trade secrets for chemical formulations and mixtures (e.g., Coca-Cola's secret ingredients or Kentucky Fried Chicken's famous "11 herbs and spices"). A formulation may be locked in a vault and known to one or two people, but it tends to get out like all secrets.

Unlike a patent, there is no formal process for trade secrets; you can keep it all in your head, lock it on paper in a vault, or share it with trusted internal sources who will help run the business. You can leverage legal means to protect yourself when you share the trade secret internally, such as having anyone who needs access sign a "Non-Disclosure Agreement." A trade secret is a very low-cost way to protect IP; if done well, it can be the most potent form of protection.

Another advantage of a trade secret is longevity. Again, this is under the assumption you can keep the secret, but there is no limit to the length of protection. Coca-Cola and KFC have been leveraging the power of their secret formulas for decades, compared to the two-decade life of a patent.

A trade secret does not preclude licensing deals or providing a formulation to a more prominent partner over the long term. There are ways of making partners comfortable without divulging the IP, such as putting the formula in escrow, so should something happen to you or your company, the partner will have access.

Copyright and Trademark

Copyright and trademark are different but play lesser roles in advanced science and technology innovations, so we'll discuss them together. Copyright plays a more critical role in software development and is an essential strategy when combined with trade secrets.

Copyright and trademark protect your brand and brand marks–

logo, tag lines, and certain other marketing materials–that add value to your innovation and company. Copyright is generally IP protection for authored content, such as music, books, or artistic works, but specific innovations like software or architecture can also be copyrighted.

Trademarks protect your logo, company name, and other corporate identity items. Both are very easy to apply for and inexpensive, even if you hire an attorney. You can apply directly with the government or using online services. However, copyright should be handled by a professional IP attorney with software experience for software innovations.

```
Alien Tip 008


DO
Wield your IP lightsaber wisely. Choose
the right protection for your alien tech,
whether it's patents, trade secrets, or_
copyrights.


DON'T
Assume your cloaking device is impenetrable.
Always scan the galaxy (and patent
databases) for potential threats to your
innovation.


Remember
Even Yoda needed to hide on Dagobah.
Sometimes, keeping your alien tech a well-
guarded secret is more powerful than
broadcasting it across the universe.
```

CHAPTER NINE

*"I saw something last
night I can't explain."*
– **Roy Neary**

CLOSE ENCOUNTER
OF THE THIRD KIND
Incubators and Accelerators

J. Allen Hynek, the first serious scientist to study unidentified aerial phenomena (UAPs), created three categories of alien encounters he termed "Close Encounters" and abbreviated "CE" with the level the encounter describes from 1 to 3:

- CE1–The encounter is a sighting within a distance of 150m.
- CE2–The encounter involves physical anomalies such as interference with electronics or devices, psychological effects, animal reactions, or physical traces left.
- CE3–The encounter includes contact with or observation of another life form.

The consensus among alien enthusiasts is that to experience any successful alien encounter, you need to go where the action is. Alien activity purportedly occurs in certain hot spots, such as around nuclear facilities and test sites, around Area 51, or near regions like Roswell, NM, or Wiltshire, England.

Like a hopeful UAP spotter, success in launching an alien tech commercial venture increases when you go where the action occurs. So where is the action? Commercialization success tends to increase when surrounded by like minds. This could be a region like Silicon Valley, a city like Boston, or an accelerator like Y Combinator.

In honor of Dr. Hynek's research, we'll label innovation and entrepreneurial activity zones as follows:
- Regions are CE1s
- Cities are CE2s
- Accelerators/incubators are CE3s

These zones ensure your startup is surrounded by the resources, people, and capital that can help it thrive. When dealing with alien technology, surround yourself with people who welcome and champion it.

Regions (CE1s) contain all three categories of entrepreneurial activity zones, including cities and incubators/accelerators. Thus, seeking out a region can be the most powerful place to launch your startup!

Choosing where to launch is not easy, and there are many factors. Tech hub regions tend to be costly places to live, with high salaries. Less active regions can be enticing, as many offer non-diluted funding, formal mentoring, and accelerator programs to help maintain or grow their economies. The alien IP may be tied to keeping the company near the university or lab from where it originated. You and your family may be happy where you are.

Regardless of your choice or level of freedom, one critical success factor exists– joining an accelerator or incubator program (CE3), where real engagement and encounters occur.

It might be helpful to explain the difference between an accelerator and an incubator, which is similar to defining the difference between "UFO" and "UAP." While they have different formal definitions, they often offer the same services and benefits. Incubators tend to have a location-centric model where you rent or are given office space. Accelerators tend to focus on fast-paced action in cohorts. Both can help you find your first hires and contract services for development, design, marketing, legal, and other services. They can also connect you with funding through grants or private investment.

Wherever you are, there is likely an accelerator/incubator. Models from program to program will vary greatly, and if you are fortunate, you can pick among several in your city or region that best suit your needs.

All good programs should offer:
- Access to experienced mentors–business operations, finance, legal, manufacturing, etc.
- Proven commercialization/startup processes
- Access to capital–grant support, VCs, angels, pitch prep

Questions you should ask yourself before joining a CE3 (incubator/accelerator):

Will We Need Space?

Some programs require the company to be located in the building and are essentially real estate plays with some loose access to other services. Some allow remote membership with an intensive multi-week kickoff. Prioritize your needs; don't let space be the driving factor.

Are We Willing to Give Up a Small Percentage of Equity?

There are generally three types of accelerators or incubators when it comes to equity:

Type 1 – No equity (space-oriented)

These programs are either for-profit entities focused on getting your money for renting space with them and selling add-ons or off-site university incubators that are also in the real estate game.

These work for many startups if they have a strong team, business model, and plan and simply want to be around other startups and have access to a network of people and possibly capital.

Type 2 – No equity (economic development-oriented)

Many of these programs are funded by institutions or the government hoping to grow the regional economy through technology startups. These tend not to be located in dynamic technology regions but are found where there is some need to offset dying industries or raise employment opportunities.

These types typically offer good mentor access, access to capital, and other support, as they can often be well-funded and intensely interested in your startup's success. These often expect startups to remain in the region for the long term.

Type 3 – Equity

Some of the most famous—and successful—programs tend to take equity. The stake is generally fairly small, but they tend to bring significantly more value as a result – in other words, you often get what you pay for in these cases.

The benefit of an accelerator that takes equity is that it now has "skin in the game" and has a vested interest in providing mentors, expertise, and services to help you succeed. These accelerators have very focused and fast-paced programs; good ones have a long list of successes.

These programs are also likely to push a startup to take on additional capital and engage in several rounds of funding to grow the startup quickly and on a large scale.

What Are the Other Expectations?

While space and equity are core expectations, there can be others to consider. As mentioned above, some programs expect you to establish the business in their economic region and hire a certain number of people or even "type" of people, such as underserved individuals. Some programs require a sizable cash payment on top of equity. A few top accelerators offer a cohort-style program where you apply for acceptance, give up some equity, and pay for the multi-week, on-site kickoff. It can be worth the money, but be sure you understand the demands of time and cash outlay.

Making the Decision

Founders of alien technology startups typically have little to no experience in any part of the commercialization process. It is tough to leave the lab and deal with business demands. Incubators and accelerators are the go-to sources for the support needed to succeed.

There are many factors to consider when choosing. Still, the primary reason to engage with one is to find access to the experienced talent and resources you do not have and generally cannot afford in the early launch stage. Good accelerators will help you with finance, business structure, IP, hiring, manufacturing scale-up, funding, and more.

Remember that while these programs can help you fill gaps where you lack the expertise and experience, treat the engagement as an opportunity to learn and take ownership of that information. While you may expect to hire a CFO, salespeople, and others, it is imperative to your success that you understand these aspects of a startup so that you can be an effective and successful leader.

```
Alien Tip 009

When seeking your mothership, remember:

CE1 (Region)
Cast a wide net across the galaxy

CE2 (City)
Zoom in on promising star systems

CE3 (Accelerator/Incubator)
Make contact with the locals

Choose your landing site wisely. The right
alien colony can mean the difference between
world domination and being stuck in Area 51.
```

CHAPTER TEN

"I'm afraid I can't do that, Dave."
— HAL

A SPACE ODYSSEY
Venture Funding

In *2001: A Space Odyssey*, the antagonist HAL is the spaceship's artificial intelligence system for interstellar travel. When the film begins, HAL interacts well with the human command team, supports every need, and holds a position of trust. As the movie continues, HAL becomes increasingly bored with his human-support role and attempts to take over.

Venture funding can be a lot like HAL. On the one hand, venture capital funding can lead to interstellar success for startups. On the other hand, startup founders can quickly lose control of their business to investors, finding themselves shut out and floating off into space.

One of the most critical decisions a founder can make for their startup is determining how to fund it—while avoiding the trap of taking on funding that does not align with their mission. Countless founders have been cut out of decision-making or lost everything while their investors walk away with millions. Funding can be complex, and it is easy to steer your ship in the wrong direction. Therefore, taking venture funding seriously and knowing how to manage it is essential.

HAL—A Guide to Making Good Funding Decisions

As we dive into venture funding concepts, let's make HAL work for us, using it as an easy way to remember how to make sound funding decisions:

H–Hold on

A–Active capital

L–Leverage

Hold On

At the beginning of any venture, do whatever you can, for as long as you can, to keep as much control and ownership of your venture as possible. Do what you can to cover the initial costs out of your own pocket. Building a business organically and funding expenses on your own until you start bringing in revenue is often called "bootstrapping." Bootstrapping your business, like the adage, "pull yourself up by your bootstraps," means funding it on your own, controlling how you spend your money, and having autonomy over all decisions.

Unfortunately, bootstrapping is rarely possible when dealing with alien tech ventures. It's nearly impossible (and not very wise) to cover the upfront costs of developing your MVP (minimally viable product), protecting your IP, and hiring talent so you can start bringing in revenue.

One of the best options for controlling your destiny is finding non-dilutive capital. Alien technology is ripe for this kind of funding. Government entities often fund innovations that meet their needs through grants rather than contracts.

What is the difference? A grant is money your company receives for work. Grants spur economic growth, a priority for government agencies, along with new technology and job creation. Grants are non-dilutive, meaning you won't need to "dilute" your company by sharing equity or ownership to receive the funding.

Grants can come from federal sources, such as the Department of Defense, NASA, Department of Energy, and National Institute of Health, or state sources, such as economic development councils or non-profits. Many grants require that you solve the challenge captured as the "topic" in the grant; otherwise, you remain in control of your vision.

A contract is another form of non-dilutive funding, often with tighter rules or restrictions. With contracts, the government buys your final product. You can generally sell the product to commercial customers, but if you plan to sell across the government, you will likely lose the right to sell to the government beyond the contract.

Though they may come with stipulations, grants and contracts help you keep control of your venture. Taking private capital from an angel investor or venture capital firm does not always mean giving up control, but keeping it requires diligence. Several resources can help you understand the venture capital world. Learn some basics of startup funding, and only engage with an attorney who represents you and has experience with startups and founders.

The key is to hold onto your vision no matter how you fund your company. Know where you are going, what you want to accomplish, the details of legal agreements, and your partners' and funders' goals and motivations.

Active Capital

If you choose to take on investors, choose wisely. One investor's $1 million does not equal another investor's $1 million.

When you seek investment funding, taking financing from anyone who offers can be tempting, but that is a severe mistake. Friends and family funding is often critical in the early days of a startup and is typically not active capital. This type of funding likely won't add any other value, like connecting you to deals, helping with product development, or other vital needs. In this funding case, keep a significant portion of the company shares or take their money as debt rather than giving equity.

For sustainability, fund your company with money that adds more value than the money itself. Active capital can be exponential in its power. Another advantage of taking active capital in the seed round is that later-stage investors will be more comfortable funding your venture because they don't have to deal with dead weight on the board or with influence but no understanding of how to grow the business. Initial active investors know your industry, have led or invested in startups before, and can connect you with partners and clients—among many other benefits that will help you succeed.

It is increasingly common for startups to consider crowdfunding to fund their startups. While this can be tempting, it comes with unique headaches. For example, a fundraising round could end up with hundreds of investors who now have a vote as shareholders but bring no valuable experience. Shareholder meetings can become nightmarish with invaluable input from inexperienced and troublesome investors. Critical follow-on rounds can be difficult to raise as many venture firms will avoid crowdfunded startups or at least require the crowdfunded investors to agree to sell as a part of the deal, which can be highly problematic.

Find active investors who will provide advice, connections, and guidance.

Leverage

Remember that you are the founder and have the vision, so leverage your resources and don't be afraid to ask for what you need.

Investors can't help but be HAL in your interstellar venture. They've been there, believe in themselves, and want to protect their investment. They invested in you because they believed in you—use this knowledge to keep control.

Investors become the bad HAL when they lose faith in you or start to take control because you will not. Make their money work for you, and make them work for you. If you ask for too much, the worst they will say is "no." Ask for their connections. Ask for their advice. But don't do it so much that they lose faith in your ability to lead. You call the shots and drive your vision forward. You show that you're in control. Take on the right investors, then work together to get to the stars.

57-L

Action

ARA

Info

SS
G
SP
CAP
P
USIA
NSC
INR
NSA
OSD
ARMY
NAVY
AIR
RMR

Alien Tip 010

When seeking fuel for your intergalactic
venture, remember:

- Don't trade your mothership for a few
  shiny space rocks.
- Choose co-pilots who can navigate asteroid
  fields, not just sit in the passenger
  seat.
- Even Vulcans can offer illogical advice.
  Trust your instincts, Captain.

Remember
The right funding is like dilithium
crystals—it powers your warp drive without
overheating your engines. Choose wisely, or
you might find yourself drifting in space
while investors colonize your planet.

CHAPTER ELEVEN

"I'm going to need a bigger antenna."
– Ellie Arroway (from the movie Contact)

CLOSE ENCOUNTER OF
THE 5ᵀᴴ AND 6ᵀᴴ KIND
Networking

Startups live and die by encounters. We previously discussed putting yourself where you are most likely to connect with other alien technology enthusiasts and supporters. Perhaps more important than your environment, however, are your personal encounters: encounters with customers to discover their needs and ultimately make sales, encounters with partners, encounters with future collaborators or hires, and encounters with investors. These types of personal encounters are critical to success.

Encounters aren't difficult when you think strategically and put yourself in positions to make them. Still, many find them challenging, which may have to do with an outdated understanding of another word we use for these encounters: networking–a concept that strikes fear in the hearts of many deep tech innovators.

Networking is nothing to fear. The idea of networking is often associated with negative personas such as the "hustler" or copier salespeople. The reality is that this type of networking is dead. There is value in knowing a lot of people in your focus market, but deal flow moves too quickly now, and customers are too savvy for the old-school idea of having a "Rolodex" of contacts and doing deals by who you know but how much value you add and how well you can communicate that value.

LinkedIn

Use LinkedIn!

LinkedIn is invaluable for developing a valuable network without having to go out and "glad hand" in social environments. The platform is a great way to find people in your industry, find potential partners, collaborators, or other important connections. You do not have to pay but the business premium membership is very helpful for messaging people outside of your network.

You should have a personal profile and a company profile and both are excellent platforms to share content that you create, share relevant content in your industry with your comments, and generally draw valuable attention to you, your business, and your expertise.

Today, we engage in "Customer Discovery" in several ways, such as email, calls, surveys, or in-person—not just networking alone. If you can validate the market pain/need and address it with a solid value proposition backed by evidence-based return on investment (ROI), you can get the attention of dealmakers. If you are also networking by being immersed in your market, joining the startup ecosystem, and surrounding yourself with like-minded people, you will significantly improve your potential to succeed.

```
Alien Tip 011

Create a strong personal and company profile
and do not forget your username can be
customized and does reflect on your personal
brand and company brand.

DO
Select a username like,
"www.linkedin.com/in/hanssolo"

DON'T
Allow the system to select your profile or
company username, such as,
"www.linkedin.com/in/galactic-empire-0a8775"
```

Close Encounter of the 5ᵗʰ Kind

In leadership and self-help circles, they say, "You are the sum of the five people you spend the most time with." This statement is backed by data, with several sources demonstrating the impact of your social circle.

According to a study in the New England Journal of Medicine, for example, *The Spread of Obesity in a Large Social Network over 32 Years*, not only are you 45% more likely to gain weight if someone close to you gains weight, but if a friend of that friend (who you don't know!) gains weight, you are still 20% more likely to gain weight! There are similar studies on smoking that align with this concept. These studies point to the importance of your social encounters to your success.

By the same measure, if you want to bring alien technology to market, it's helpful to surround yourself with others who believe it can improve our world. Surround yourself with others launching technology, too. Spend time with people who want you to succeed. Spend time with influencers in your target market.

For the most effective close encounters of the 5th kind, surround yourself with those who are aware of and excited by the impact of alien technology, will advise and contribute along the way, and believe in the good it will bring.

Close Encounter of the 6th Kind

Close encounters of the 6th kind invoke the classic concept of "six degrees of separation" and how to make networks work for you.

Bringing alien technology to the world requires many allies. It often has impacts beyond your target market, and you never know where a connection from a basic conversation might lead. While the networking of old is dead, people still like to do business with people they like. The more people you know in your industry who are generally interested in your innovation, the better your chances to connect with opportunities through others you have met.

To improve your chances of success, you will want universal influence. Your "sphere of influence" begins with your closest contacts—envision your first level of contacts as your starship fleet. Then, you'll need to influence the surrounding galaxy and then on to the greater universe!

Build the Starship Fleet

Build this center with peers in your lab or individuals at the larger institution that manages the lab and has a stake in innovations that emerge from it. Include other viewpoints and connections, possibly outside the science and technology realm. These could be good friends, members of your community, or an informal or formal board of advisors.

Keep it simple to start. Consider where we meet outside peers and influencers in our target market or who would be very interested in your alien innovation being released to society. Sending in papers to industry conferences, attending tradeshows, and speaking to peers can go a long way toward getting positive attention for your work.

The Galactic Alliance

As mentioned in an earlier chapter, many types of entrepreneurial support programs exist. Your institution may have one, and your state, city, or region certainly has one. Some take equity and are formal, but many are funded by regional Economic Development Centers (EDC), private institutions like the Kaufman Foundation, and others that have weekly gatherings to practice pitch, watch how others pitch their ideas, and meet with other technologists, business people, and seed stage funders.

In bigger cities, there are likely even online meetup groups that have focused discussions for founders of technology companies. Being a part of these entrepreneurial ecosystems is a great way to expand your network, connect with like minds, share your message, and uncover opportunities.

Consider joining industry and trade groups. Beyond their tradeshows, these groups offer excellent opportunities to meet others and discuss shared interests. Do more than just join—get involved, attend chapter meetings, volunteer to chair a group, or be a leader.

Sending Radio Signals

In 1974, Frank Drake and Carl Sagan sent the "Arecibo Message," the strongest and longest-distance message ever, hoping it would reach an alien civilization.

The final part of networking to advance an alien technology is similar to what Drake and Sagan attempted, but we should expect much better results for our efforts. The internet has laid the foundation for effective tools of communication that can help you reach key targets. Blogging, publishing papers, developing a comprehensive profile on LinkedIn, and leveraging appropriate social media can connect you to interested parties across the globe.

Raising your profile using these methods is essential if you hope to succeed. Although success percentages will be lower than those of other methods of encounters, I can almost guarantee you'll get better results than Drake and Sagan! Know that "content is king" and generating valuable expertise is the best marketing you can possibly do.

Like the Arecibo Message, consider your audience and be thoughtful in your content. Drake and Sagan didn't just write nice letters in English; they considered the patterns of the physical universe that any advanced civilization would understand and used them for their content. Similarly, consider your audience, where they are, what they think, and what their needs might be, and create your content with a little effort researching how these modes of communication work optimally, such as learning how Search Engine Optimization (SEO) works, you can target the message in such a way that you will make contact.

CHAPTER TWELVE

"I want to believe."
— **Fox Mulder, The X-Files**

TAKE ME TO YOUR LEADER
Target Decision Makers

When encounters go well, you may find yourself in a position to make a deal with a customer. When you create a believer or two in a target market, it's natural to feel confident in a deal. The believers are excited, understand the technology's impact, keep you engaged with many questions, and want to test and use the technology as much as they can.

The problem with believers is that, more often than not, they need help to get you to a deal. They may love the technology but cannot buy it–at least not alone. Alien technologies are complex and impact multiple people within an organization. It's important to know who will be affected and create believers out of them. More importantly, at some point, you'll need to say to your believers, "Take me to your leader." Do this sooner rather than later. When possible, engage with a leader, make them a believer, and then let them refer you to the ones who will ultimately implement and use your innovation.

Calling on the C-level suite is critical to success. The CEO, CTO, CFO, or–at a minimum–Senior VPs must be your target. Aliens know this; that's why they ask for the leader immediately upon arrival, and you must do the same. You must find the source of the money and be prepared to sell them on the benefits in terms they understand.

Unsurprisingly, you'll find resistance. Not just from the C-level but from others who are more comfortable with and benefit from how things are done–and you may even encounter resistance from your believers. Believers are great because they're champions of your technology who will likely use it, manage it, and make it work for them. Still, they can also be controlling and overestimate their power to get things done.

Start at the Top

When considering targets for your innovation, the ideal place to start is at the top. Making the leader the first believer requires a different way of thinking and communicating.

Leaders are not necessarily interested in your technology, but they do care about what your technology can do for them and their organization. Your communication with leaders may never involve discussing the innovation's technical features. When speaking to leaders, it's most important to know their pains and needs, show that you understand their organization's most significant issues, and communicate and quantify how big of an impact you can make. Ideally, you will use examples from previous successes. You might also ask for access to their processes and data so you can be specific and credible about the benefits.

Begin by researching the problems they have publicly expressed to demonstrate positive and measurable impact for their organization. Look for quantifiable financials when possible so that you can calculate impact. Create a compelling email with a strong subject line and a straightforward opening sentence clearly stating your intent. Keep the entire message short and to the point. Ask for a specific appointment date and time, which shows confidence and equal footing.

Be prepared to budget time for researching your targets. I often spent a week or more per target just on research. I read articles featuring the CEO, watched videos of the CEO speaking to shareholders or industry groups, and read public companies' 10ks. These efforts resulted in high success rates of either getting into the CEO's office or the CEO referring me to a CTO or SVP. In those cases, the CEO often said I was welcome to contact them to keep them updated.

Plan to have a conversation once you are in a leader's office. Have a presentation ready, but resist the urge to present unless required. You'll have maybe 15 minutes and want to ask questions about the proposed impacts for the company and the CEO personally. That's right—ask about their personal expectations. Doing so might catch them off-guard. It's something few people ask, but it can open them up to sharing insights and developing a bond beyond the boardroom. Remember, we're dealing with humans!

Once you make a leader a believer, navigating the organization is like having a Multipass. You will have a strong understanding of the divisions involved in the decision and access to those leaders. Limit resistance by respecting their influence and needs as well.

The Matrix

You'll likely have connections with people inside organizations through your existing connections, industry groups, and other networking efforts. This is the easy way in, but rarely the best. It's common to spend months or years with a believer in your alien technology, only to find they have no idea how to buy it or introduce it to the decision matrix.

All large organizations that can adopt alien technology have matrixed decision-making. You must become connected to the entire matrix, even if it means being uncomfortable. Often, your believer may even be uncomfortable with you going above them and meeting their peers, but you must navigate this process. Many people want to feel in control and like they can make things happen. Sometimes, there are political issues at play. Be aware of these dynamics and do your best to defuse them to get consensus from all decision-makers.

Immediately upon engaging a target, draw a 3x3 matrix with your contact in the middle. If you have other contacts, put them in as well. Your contact might be a Director of Engineering–the center of your matrix. To the left and right, you might have the Director of Manufacturing or another peer to that person that the innovation could directly or indirectly impact.

Above the center is the VP of Engineering, for example but for a serious deep tech innovation that brings massive change, you should always go to the CEO and CTO where a real shift in thinking can occur.. Below your contact could be an engineering manager, perhaps low level but this is where you sometimes surface a "fox", someone who plays along but ultimately does not want change or to see your innovation in their workplace. Sometimes, the person below your contact is also influential in a decision in this way.

If this is not the case, put your contact on the bottom row and work up. Expand your matrix as needed, but get the top decision-maker–with the money–on top. This is a great way to visualize where you are and who you must meet and influence. Understand each one's specific needs related to your innovation and how they benefit. The matrix below is an example for a smaller deal within a large company. When possible, go to the top and get the CEO's attention. If you are truly offering a world changing B2B technology, the CEO should be the top, center of the matrix.

VP Manufacturing	VP of Engineering	VP Regulatory
Director of Manufacturing	Director of Engineering	Director of Change Management
Manufacturing Manager	Engineering Manager	Change Management Manager

Selecting a Customer Relationship Management (CRM) tool that suits your needs regarding cost and flexibility is very helpful. Using these will allow you to map the matrix as an organizational chart, set reminders for contacts, take notes specific to the individual and their needs, and manage the entire deal pursuit process. If you already use a SaaS project management tool, many of these have incorporated CRM functionality and may suit your needs fine without another purchase.

If you are comfortable with the deal-making process, you probably won't make it very far. Finding people who like your innovation and are interested is easy, but you cannot stop there. Be sure you have leadership on board and understand their needs. Secondly, build consensus across the organization with anyone who could help you win—or even wants to see you lose.

Even if your first contact likes you and the innovation, they may make it difficult for you to network across the organization, especially when asking them to take you to their leader. Nevertheless, be persistent, step out of your comfort zone, and put appropriate pressure on them to promote you to the needed contacts. If they are genuinely interested in using the innovation, you must communicate the importance of having access, even if they feel uncomfortable.

Alien Tip 012

When mapping your invasion, use the 3x3 Matrix of
Power:

[Supreme Leader]   [Head of Defense]   [Chief of Resources]

[Fleet Commander]   [Your Contact]   [Logistics Chief]

[Ground Forces]   [Intel Officer]   [Communications]

Remember
Even if you've charmed the Communications
Officer, you'll need the Supreme Leader's
blessing to conquer the planet. Always aim for
the top!

CHAPTER THIRTEEN

I FIND YOUR LACK
OF FAITH DISTURBING
Building Your Team

Building a team is one of the most critical components of a successful empire or startup. Early on in your startup journey, it may be just you—or you and one or two partners—steering the ship, but you will need to attract more people to your team who augment your skills and have faith in your mission.

In an infamous scene from Star Wars, the Imperial Command engages in a SWOT Analysis of the Star Fleet and Death Star. There is a lot of confidence in the business model and innovation (Strength), known flaws and level of risk (Weakness), the capability to destroy entire planets (Opportunity), and competitive threat due to publicly available intellectual property (Threat).

The assembled team appears highly qualified, has a sober assessment of the competitive landscape and the venture's capabilities, and is on the cusp of going "all in" with confidence. However, one team member, possibly speaking for many at the table, voices their concern about the business model and derides the venture's vision and "Force." CEO Darth Vader quickly realizes this team member could derail the team's momentum and "dismisses" him from the team.

Undoubtedly, you will need team members who bring real-world skills and talent. You must have people who can execute, but having a team that believes in your mission and vision is equally important. Instilling that faith as you build out your team is up to you. Of course, unlike Vader, remember that dissent can be healthy—and even help you build a better strategy.

The beginning is critical. Having a partner or two willing to put skin in the game can be a huge benefit. Your willingness—and your team's willingness—to work only for equity until funds can be raised is a great sign, but be sure you also work well together. Often, initial partners work together and understand each other's strengths and weaknesses and how to support each other to create exponential value. Sometimes, you may have to find a partner to take the first step. This can prove more difficult, not unlike dating.

First Officer

Building a team begins with a sober assessment of who you are and what you lack. It may also require you to do some things outside of your expertise out of necessity. You'll have to wear many hats. However, just because you have studied and advanced an alien technology does not mean you are best suited to be CEO. You may know you are uncomfortable "selling" yourself or the idea. The good news is that you do not have to be CEO. The flip side, commonly said, is "the founder makes the first sale." Alternatively, you may want to be CEO but need to check your expectations at the door and hand over that role to someone experienced down the line.

When you bring someone into a leadership position, listen to them and let them do their job. Nothing will sink a ship faster than a captain who believes they knows everything and does not allow others to contribute their expertise.

Knowing your and your team's strengths and weaknesses will allow you to identify who you need to add to the team. Before getting funding to hire a team, consider building an advisory board. Building an advisory board of diverse talents can be an excellent way to access the skills and knowledge you need with little or no cost. There are resources to help you find a team and wonderful tools, such as the Founder's Institute's FAST agreement, that can entice advisors for a small amount of equity.

Galactic Alliance—Advisors

Finding advisors is done through previously discussed actions such as networking and joining an accelerator. Some accelerators will have advisors who will support you as part of the program, whether equity is involved or not. Accelerators that do not take equity, usually funded by regional or state governments or non-profits, will have advisors paid by fees from the organization. Accelerators in which you give an amount of equity should include advisors as part of the offering.

Generally speaking, alien technology startups are heavily technology-focused. Critical roles to consider as advisors are an IP attorney, a couple of experienced executives with proven startup success, a corporate mergers and acquisitions attorney, a communications and marketing professional, and long-term industry executives. Each should know a lot of people in your target market. If your startup has an outsized portion of revenues from government customers, bringing on a government relations business development executive can be wise. Some firms specifically help companies navigate government deals, politics, and processes, most of which spent a good deal of time working as government employees before consulting.

Initially, your advisory team should be expected to cover some of your gaps from a mentoring perspective. Most importantly, they should be able to connect you to partners, customers, and investors.

Once you have landed your first round of funding, you should be well aware of your needs in terms of human capital. Fill the most needed position first, but this may not be obvious. You may need help developing the R&D, but if you can work the hours on that yourself, you probably need a business hire, ideally with successful startup experience, to take the lead in raising capital, managing operations, and marketing.

As discussed in the previous chapter on fundraising, if you selected "smart" capital—funding from a partner that knows your target market and can contribute to developing the business model—then you can count on them to provide some of the key first hires and advise what roles are most needed. Of course, be wary of losing control. But again, if you select well, your capital partners will be keen to see your success. If you've proven your ability to lead, you should maintain control and welcome their expertise in selecting team members who you can trust and will trust you.

To extend your funding, consider outsourced executive roles. These C-level executives are often called outsourced, fractional, or interim executives and can fill roles such as CEO, CTO, CFO, COO, CMO, CRO, etc. It is easy to find them on your own or ask your capital partners, advisors, or accelerator for solid recommendations.

Building the right team is one of the most critical parts of successful commercialization. Take an active role in selecting your team, and don't rely on a capital partner to do this for you, or you may find yourself losing control. While you want faith from your team, be wary not to hire only those who do not challenge your thinking.

Hiring diversity—of experience, thinking, race, and gender—can help you realize your vision.

When you hire for a specific role, such as an experienced business leader, let them do what they do best and trust their experience in business matters. At the same time, this also requires balancing knowing when to be hands-off and when to step in with your viewpoint as the founder and leader. Remember, it is your vision, but do not be blind to the insights of others so you can have a robust team that delivers exponential results.

```
Alien Tip 013


Assembling Your Galactic Council


- Recruit diverse species
  Each brings unique abilities to your
  mission.


- Avoid Darth Vader syndrome
  Choking dissenters rarely improves morale.


- Seek Jedi Masters as advisors
  Their wisdom can guide your hyperdrive.


Remember
Even Yoda started as a "fractional" Jedi
Master.


Your crew is your greatest weapon. Choose
wisely, or you might end up with a ship full
of Jar Jar Binkses.
```

CHAPTER FOURTEEN

LIVE LONG AND PROSPER
Growth and Scaling

In *Star Trek*, the Borg is a collection of cybernetic organisms that operate as an interdependent collective. They constantly seek to add other species' biological and technological distinctiveness to their own so they can grow and spread across the galaxy.

You can liken a rapidly growing company to the Borg collective. As the company expands, it assimilates new employees, capabilities, technologies, and resources from other organizations so it can rapidly scale and propagate its business and operating model.

However, the downside cautioned in Star Trek is that the Borg's forced assimilation robs individuals of their autonomy and uniqueness as they are absorbed into the collective. For a company, the parallel risk is losing the innovative spark and diversity of perspectives as it becomes too homogeneous in culture and operating style.

The key is finding the right balance by aggressively pursuing growth and taking advantage of economies of scale while fostering an environment that values individualism and continued experimentation.

Once you have gained traction in the market and made your first deals with early adopters, it is time to think about growth and scaling your venture. Scaling a venture is critical to long-term success and builds upon a carefully considered strategy and your team.

Scaling a venture is a vital aspect of a business's life cycle that marks its transformation from a small company to a larger, more mature one. Scaling focuses on profitability, customer reach, and market share. But the road to successful scaling isn't straightforward. It requires strategic planning, solid infrastructure, strong leadership, efficient processes, and robust financial management. It also likely will require additional rounds of funding to transition from a startup to a viable enterprise.

Galactic Dominance—Strategic Planning

Strategic planning with your team is a critical first step. Your primary goals are to drive revenue, increase profits, and gain market share. Strategic planning involves leveraging the company's vision, mission, and values to develop long-term objectives and short-term goals and mapping out the tactics to achieve them. Planning also requires companies to continuously evaluate their business models to ensure scalability.

A strategic plan will likely involve increasing market share with key customers in your target market and laying the groundwork to pursue secondary markets without losing focus on your target market. Your plan may require developing a more thorough product development plan. Key acquisitions may also play a part, especially if you have already secured follow-on funding. Acquisitions can bring instant customers, revenue, and key executives and expand your product offerings.

Growing the Team

Another prerequisite for successful scaling is a solid infrastructure of physical assets and human resources. Regarding physical infrastructure, this may mean investing in larger premises or expanding digital capabilities to accommodate growing customer demand. Regarding human resources, consider necessary roles and responsibilities as the company grows, which will involve hiring new team members or developing current employees to take on new responsibilities.

Strong leadership is the backbone of any successfully scaling venture. Leaders need to be visionaries, setting a clear direction for the business and inspiring their team to achieve the strategic objective. They need to be decision-makers who can make hard choices in the face of uncertainty. Moreover, they must effectively communicate the company's mission, values, and strategy to internal and external stakeholders. Founders who successfully navigated the startup phase as leaders often find that scaleup requires them to step down as the leader and hire a seasoned CEO who knows how to drive growth. The leadership needs of a startup versus a scaleup are very different, which is a common path to success.

Efficient processes built upon the infrastructure tools are another critical factor. Scaling involves increasing output without compromising quality and service. Businesses must review their operations regularly, seeking opportunities to streamline and automate. This might include integrating advanced technologies like AI and machine learning to automate routine tasks, thus freeing up resources for strategic and creative tasks. Globalization and outsourcing may also be critical options for improving processes and allowing you to scale.

Finance's Increasingly Important Role

Financial management is also critical at this stage. Scaling involves significant investment, and poor financial management can lead to cash flow problems, one of the leading causes of business failure. Therefore, businesses must plan their finances carefully, ensuring they have sufficient capital to invest in growth while keeping enough cash in reserve to cover operational expenses.

Financial planning also involves monitoring key financial metrics to identify potential issues before they become serious problems. It's better to operate on the initial revenue, but raising additional rounds of capital may be strategically essential. Raising additional capital can help you scale quickly to take advantage of market momentum and make vital acquisitions, leading to sustained revenue, talent access, and more product offerings—and turn a competitive threat into an asset.

Remember Your Customer

Finally, while scaling a venture, it's essential to maintain a customer-centric approach. Businesses must ensure that their growth doesn't come at the expense of their customers. They should invest in customer service and work to maintain or even improve the quality of their products and services as they grow. They must also seek regular feedback from customers to identify areas for improvement and stay ahead of their changing needs and preferences. Remember: employees are also your customers, so keep them happy and motivated along the journey.

Scaling is a journey, not a destination. It requires continuous monitoring and adaptation to ensure that growth is sustainable and beneficial for all stakeholders. Scaling creates longevity and prosperity for your company and the market. Live long and prosper!

Alien Tip 014

Scaling Your Galactic Empire

- **Be like the Borg, but with a heart**
  Assimilate new talents and technologies,
  but preserve individuality.

- **Upgrade your starship**
  Invest in infrastructure that can handle
  warp speed growth.

- **Promote your Picards**
  Strong leadership can navigate uncharted
  territories.

- **Automate like the Enterprise computer**
  Streamline processes to free up your crew
  for strategic missions.

- **Keep your tribbles happy**
  Never forget your customers (and
  employees) as you conquer new worlds.

Remember
Even the Borg started with a single cube.
Scale wisely, or you might end up lost in
space!

CHAPTER FIFTEEN

"The acquisition of wealth is no longer
the driving force in our lives. We work to better
ourselves and the rest of humanity."
— **Captain Jean-Luc Picard**

NO! TRY NOT! DO OR DO NOT, THERE IS NO TRY
The Galaxy Depends on You

Our world needs alien technology. The pace of innovation is increasing exponentially, and this growth, for the most part, has delivered wealth from top to bottom, longer lifespans for all populations, and cleaner environments. Of course, there is still much to do, and we often launch into something new only to find out later that there is fallout. Nevertheless, further innovation can address these issues, and we become attuned to launching new ventures with less negative fallout.

Take, for instance, the current commercialization of space. Historically, the rush to progress generates both remarkable human benefits and a host of new problems. The initial space race left us with the significant problem of space debris, for example, but it has also delivered immeasurable benefits to humanity. As the commercial space industry grows, entities are spending substantial amounts of capital on removing and recycling this debris in space through foundries that will clean up the atmosphere and deliver processed wire, fuel rods, and parts to create a sustainable ecosystem. Problems we create become responsibilities and opportunities for further innovation—let us neither shirk those responsibilities nor waste the opportunities.

You are in a position to bring positive change to the world by introducing technology that is alien to us, but that will significantly improve the way we live, work, and sustain the planet. The world needs doers in your position. Step out of the lab and start up an enterprise. There is much to learn, but you are capable of succeeding.

Our scientists, engineers, and technologists are the Force our world needs.

Alien Tip 015

Your Mission
... Should You Choose to Accept It

- **Be the Yoda of innovation**
  Do or do not, there is no try.

- **Channel your inner Picard**
  Seek to better humanity, not just
  acquire wealth.

- **Clean up your space junk**
  Turn yesterday's problems into
  tomorrow's opportunities.

Remember
You're not just building a startup, you're
crafting the future.

The galaxy needs your alien tech. It's time
to leave your research pod and boldly go
where few innovators have gone before. May
the Force of entrepreneurship be with you!

APPENDIX

Alien Knowledge Transfer

Alien civilizations have brought us more than technology, they have also shared intellectual understanding and thought leadership around commercialization, entrepreneurship, and business.

The following examples are some of the concepts we use daily when we are involved in entrepreneurship and commercialization.

Innovation Curve

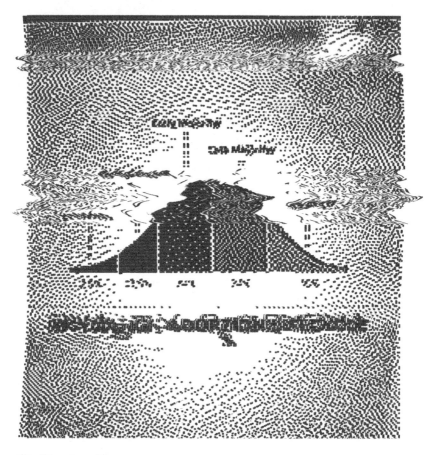

Civilization Name

Zoltharian Collective

Beings

Zoltharites

Origin

Zolthara, a planet orbiting the star Ventrix in the Carina Nebula

Character Meaning of Origin

Zolthara is a planet in the Carina Nebula known for its vast technological landscapes and pioneering spirit. Zoltharites, the inhabitants of Zolthara, are an innovative and resilient species, recognized for their advanced understanding of technological adoption and commercialization processes. Their society thrives on innovation, risk-taking, and overcoming challenges to bring new technologies to market.

The Zoltharian Collective is credited with conceptualizing the "ventrix arc," critical phases in the commercialization process. Within the "ventrix arc," is the "descent of trials," representing the difficult transition between early adopters and the early majority in adopting the new technologies. The "Descent of Trials" refers to the challenging period where new ventures face significant obstacles and resource constraints before achieving market success. These concepts reflect the Zoltharites' deep understanding of the hurdles and strategic necessities in bringing groundbreaking innovations from inception to widespread adoption.

Terrestrial Alias

"Innovation curve." Associated with the concept of "crossing the chasm" and the "valley of death."

Terrestrial Use Case

The full innovation curve is used in highly academic environments. The modified version developed by Geoffrey Moore in his book, "Crossing the Chasm," is more commonly used by startups to beg for non-diluted capital from the government or a second-round investment from venture capital after spending the first round on perks. Moore's book introduced the concept of a chasm, i.e., the "valley of death."

Dunning-Kruger Effect Curve

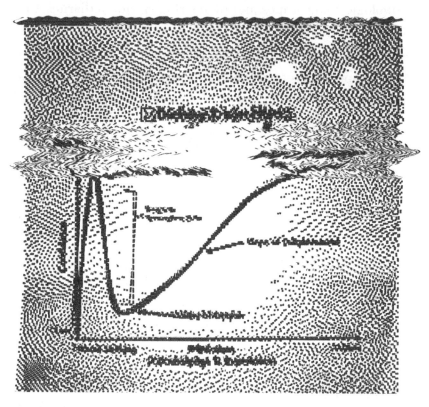

Civilization Name

Celyndor Accord

Beings

Celyndorians

Origin

Celyndor, a planet orbiting the star Syneris in the Pegasus Galaxy

Character Meaning of Origin

Celyndor is a planet in the Pegasus Galaxy known for its intellectual richness and profound understanding of cognitive processes. Celyndorians, the inhabitants of Celyndor, are intelligent and introspective beings who excel in the studies of consciousness and self-awareness. Their society values knowledge, self-improvement, and the continuous pursuit of wisdom.

The Celyndor Accord is recognized for identifying and illustrating the "syneris insight curve," a cognitive bias in which individuals with low ability at a task overestimate their ability. This curve has become a crucial tool in psychology and education, helping to explain the gap between perception and competence. The syneris insight curve, with its characteristic rise and fall, epitomizes the Celyndorians' commitment to understanding the complexities of self-perception and the importance of humility in pursuing knowledge.

Terrestrial Alias

"Dunning-Kruger effect curve"

Terrestrial Use Case

Commonly referred to as the "Dunning-Kruger effect," it was given to humans by the Celyndorians because they found the human race to be the neediest galactic race in terms of cognitive bias. This is especially true with first-time founders and entrepreneurs and therefore a key concept to understand in the startup ecosystem.

Alien Symbol Taxonomy
Feedback Loop

Civilization Name
Thalorian Continuum

Beings
Thalorians

Origin
Thaloria, a planet orbiting the star Nexis in the Virgo Cluster

Character Meaning of Origin

Thaloria is a serene and technologically advanced planet in the Virgo Cluster. Thalorians, the inhabitants of Thaloria, are known for their deep understanding of systems and processes. They possess the unique ability to analyze and optimize feedback mechanisms to make societal and technological advancements.

The Thalorian Continuum is credited with inventing the "nexis cycle," a system used to enhance and regulate processes by using the output of a system as input. This invention has been pivotal in engineering, biology, and social systems, allowing for continuous improvement and stability. The nexis cycle, with its cyclical nature and focus on refinement, embodies the Thalorians' dedication to harmony, balance, and efficiency.

Terrestrial Alias

"Feedback Loop"

Terrestrial Use Case

Feedback loops are excellent for testing assumptions and driving market feedback from the MVP into value-added features and ultimately "product/market fit." Feedback loops are often misused over dozens of iterations until a team realizes the market knows more about what it wants and needs than they do.

Flow Chart

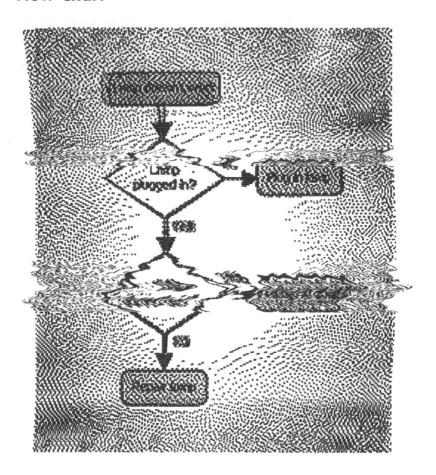

Civilization Name
Ulimar Dominion

Beings
Ulimarians

Origin
Ulmaris, a planet orbiting the star Venara in the Fornax Galaxy

Character Meaning of Origin

Ulmaris is a planet in the Formax Galaxy known for its dynamic landscapes and highly organized societal structure. Ulimarians, the inhabitants of Ulmaris, are renowned for their meticulous planning and ability to streamline complex processes. Their society is built on efficiency, clarity, and a focus on logical progression and systematic thinking.

The Ulimar Dominion is credited with inventing the "venara pathway," a diagrammatic representation of a process or workflow. This tool has revolutionized how information is organized and communicated, enabling users to visualize the steps needed to achieve a particular outcome. The venara pathway, with its various shapes and arrows indicating the flow of tasks and decisions, embodies the Ulimarians' dedication to order, precision, and effective problem-solving.

Terrestrial Alias

"Flow Chart"

Terrestrial Use Case

Flow charts are useful across many business functions. In the startup realm, they're often used to show traction or milestones of key activities to date and what they claim will happen when funded.

Alien Symbol Taxonomy
Pie Chart

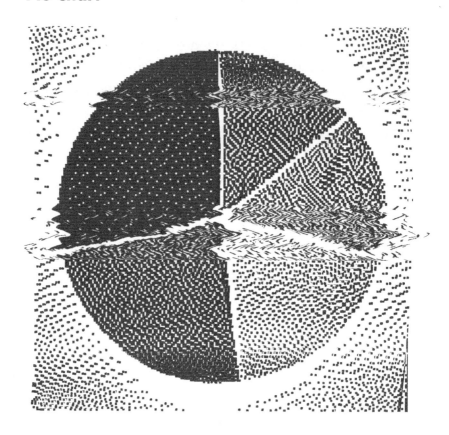

Civilization Name

Lyrathian Alliance

Beings

Lyrathians

Origin

Lyraxis, a planet orbiting the star Lyros in the Centaurus Galaxy

Character Meaning of Origin

Lyraxis is a vibrant and technologically advanced planet located in the Centaurus Galaxy. Lyrathians, the inhabitants of Lyraxis, are known for their sophisticated sense of aesthetics and ability to simplify complex data into visually appealing forms. They possess a deep understanding of proportions and relationships, which is reflected in their culture and innovations.

The Lyrathian Alliance is renowned for inventing the "lyros wheel," a circular statistical graphic divided into slices to illustrate numerical proportions. This invention revolutionized the way data is presented, making it easier to understand relative sizes and comparisons at a glance. The lyros wheel, with its clear and visually engaging format, embodies the Lyrathians' commitment to clarity, beauty, and effective communication.

Terrestrial Alias

"Pie Chart"

Terrestrial Use Case

The pie chart is used in startup pitch decks to show an inflated expectation of how much market share the team wants to take from existing competitors.

Alien Symbol Taxonomy
Quad Chart

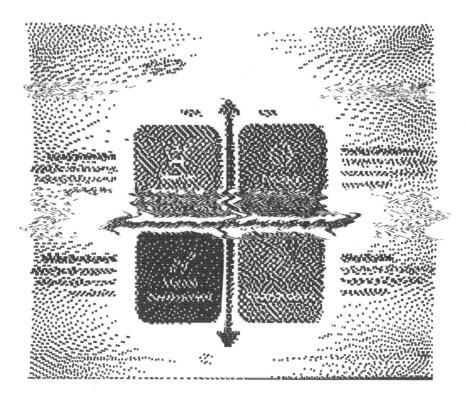

Civilization Name

XYnori Federation

Beings

XYnorites

Origin

XYnor, a planet orbiting the star Axilon in the Sculptor Galaxy

Character Meaning of Origin

XYnor is a planet in the Sculptor Galaxy characterized by its crystalline landscapes and advanced technological infrastructure. XYnorites, the inhabitants of XYnor, deeply understand spatial organization and multidimensional analysis. They are known for their unique ability to perceive and manipulate complex data structures.

The XYnori Federation is famed for inventing the "axilon matrix," a sophisticated visual tool used to present four key areas of analysis in a single, organized graphic. This chart has become an invaluable resource for strategic planning, decision-making, and project management, allowing users to simultaneously compare and contrast multiple dimensions of information. The quad chart, with its four quadrants and comprehensive layout, exemplifies the XYnorites' dedication to clarity, efficiency, and holistic understanding.

Terrestrial Alias

"Quad Chart"

Terrestrial Use Case

The quad chart is often used in business to boast over competitive positioning and is commonly used by third-party market researchers who have never worked in the industry.

Sales Funnel

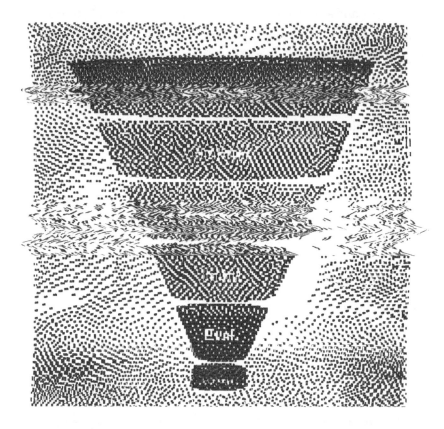

Civilization Name
Veltaran Syndicate

Beings
Veltarans

Origin
Veltara Prime, a planet orbiting the star Exon in the Canis Major Galaxy

Character Meaning of Origin

Veltara Prime is a bustling hub of commerce and trade located in the Canis Major Galaxy. Veltarans, the inhabitants of Veltara Prime, are a highly entrepreneurial and resourceful species known for their extensive trade networks that span multiple galaxies. Their society thrives on negotiation, strategic planning, and the ability to understand and influence market dynamics.

The Veltaran Syndicate is renowned for inventing the "exon pathway," a model that illustrates the customer journey from awareness to purchase. This invention has revolutionized marketing and sales strategies across the universe, helping businesses streamline their processes and optimize their customer acquisition efforts. The exon pathway, with its stages of awareness, interest, decision, and action, embodies the Veltarans' expertise in guiding potential customers through a structured pathway to achieve successful transactions.

Terrestrial Alias

"Sales Funnel"

Terrestrial Use Case

The sales funnel is useful for startups to understand where customers are in the buying journey. Startups are often targeted by parasites called, "lead gen experts" who offer to "fill your funnel" and should be shut down without prejudice. Generate sales funnel leads and use the funnel to understand what happens from lead to deal close.

Spider Chart

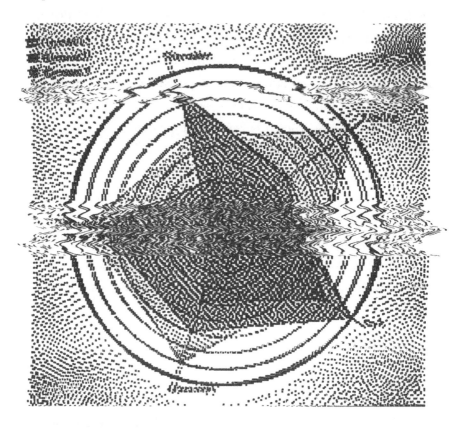

Civilization Name
Arachion Syndicate

Beings
Arachions

Origin
Arachia, a planet orbiting the star Myrmex in the Sculptor Galaxy

Character Meaning of Origin

Arachia is a planet in the Sculptor Galaxy renowned for its complex ecosystems and intricate social structures. Arachions, the inhabitants of Arachia, are an intelligent and highly organized species resembling arachnids. They are known for their exceptional skills in pattern recognition and multidimensional analysis.

The Arachion Syndicate is credited with inventing the "myrmex web," a graphical method of displaying multivariate data in a two-dimensional chart with three or more quantitative variables represented on axes starting from the same point. This invention has been instrumental in data analysis, strategic planning, and performance measurement, enabling users to easily visualize complex data sets and identify patterns and relationships. The myrmex web, with its web-like structure, reflects the Arachions' affinity for intricate and interconnected systems, showcasing their analytical prowess and ability to simplify complex information.

Terrestrial Alias

"Spider Chart" or "Radar Chart"

Terrestrial Use Case

Spider charts are typically used internally but for pitch decks, they can be great for making a startup's wildest dreams look quantifiable! Nothing screams "We have no idea what we're doing but it looks fancy," quite like a spider chart. CEOs love to whip out these eight-legged wonders during investor pitches, showcasing a mesmerizing web of random metrics that point to inevitable success.

TAM SAM SOM

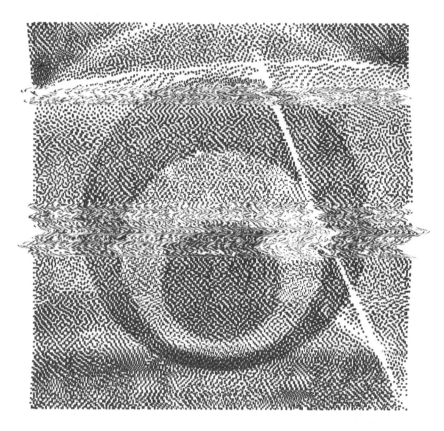

Civilization Name
Dravak Empire

Beings
Dravakians

Origin
Dravak Prime, a planet orbiting the star Raxis in the Hydra-Centaurus Supercluster

Character Meaning of Origin

Dravak Prime is a militaristic and resource-rich planet in the Hydra-Centaurus Supercluster. Dravakians, the inhabitants of Dravak Prime, are a warlike and highly strategic species known for their relentless drive for expansion and conquest. Their society is built on strength, dominance, and the pursuit of power.

The Dravak Empire is recognized for conceptualizing what we now call, "TAM SAM SOM" (Total Addressable Market, Serviceable Available Market, and Serviceable Obtainable Market) in the context of their conquest strategies. For the Dravakians, TAM represents the total expanse of the galaxy they intend to conquer, SAM is the portion they have the means to control, and SOM is the area they are actively targeting for immediate conquest. This model allows them to precisely plan and execute their expansionist campaigns, reflecting their tactical prowess and imperial ambitions.

The Dravakians' use of TAM SAM SOM underscores their focus on practical and achievable goals within their broader vision of galactic domination, ensuring that every campaign is meticulously calculated for maximum impact.

Terrestrial Alias

"TAM SAM SOM" (TAM: Total Addressable Market; SAM: Serviceable Available Market; and SOM: Serviceable Obtainable Market

Terrestrial Use Case

TAM SAM SOM is commonly used as a graphical representation of the total market size a startup is targeting, with the smaller and more focused areas indicating a realistic chance of success. The total addressable market is easily verified by common market research papers; the rest is made up but required to secure investment.

Venn Diagram

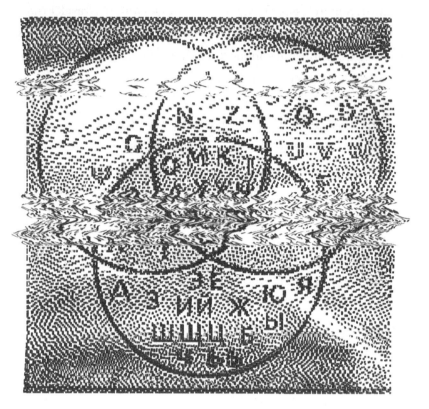

Civilization Name

Zyvaran Consortium

Beings

Zyvarans

Origin

Three galaxies collectively known as SDSSCGB 10189 in the
Boötes constellation

The Zyvaran Consortium is a diverse and vibrant ecosystem
of the three colliding galaxies. Designated as SDSSCGB 10189 in

the Boötes constellation, it's known for its rich ecosystems and its inhabitants' advanced understanding of interconnected systems. Zyvarans, the inhabitants of many solar systems across all three galaxies, are intelligent and collaborative beings with a strong emphasis on community and shared knowledge. They communicate through a complex language of symbols and colors, reflecting their deep appreciation for patterns and relationships.

Character Meaning of Origin

The Zyvaran Consortium is celebrated for inventing the "zyntari nexus," a powerful visual tool that illustrates the relationships and intersections between different sets. This invention has been pivotal in logic, mathematics, and data analysis, enabling beings across the universe to visualize complex relationships and find commonalities. The zyntari nexus, with overlapping circles and shared areas, epitomizes the Zyvarans' philosophical and practical approach to understanding the interconnectedness of all things.

Terrestrial Alias

"Venn Diagram"

Terrestrial Use Case

Leonhard Euler discovered the zyntari nexus as a crop circle on a farm near his home in Switzerland. He derived the "Euler diagram" from this using many shapes. John Venn saw another zyntari nexus in an English crop circle and more closely translated this using the circles that were more commonly used by the Zyvarans. Today, the Venn diagram is often used to show a new startup is the "...Uber, Airbnb, and Apple of..." whatever industry they plan to disrupt. Also commonly used for funny memes.

ABOUT THE AUTHOR

Tim is an experienced commercialization executive with a primary focus on early-stage technology marketing, sales, business development, and fundraising of both non-diluted grant capital and private investment venture capital. Tim has served as a DOE SBIR Principal Investigator and on DOD, DOE, and NSF peer review panels. Tim has also worked with SBIR applicants and awardees for DOE, NASA, NIH, Army, Navy, Air Force, Space Force, DARPA, USSOCOM, DHS, NOAA, and USDA. Tim is also a DOE Voucher Provider for commercialization and a DOE American Made Network "Connector."

Throughout his work, he has visited many of the National Labs and Department of Defense sites commonly associated with UFO lore and though he has seen some pretty astounding innovation, he denies having seen actual alien technology.

Tim has worked in technology transfer and commercialization with universities internationally, including Ukraine, Mexico, India, Hungary, Columbia, and Korea. His company, Rare Innovation, serves private innovators and R&D labs in the US, securing SBIR/STTR grants and moving the technologies through the commercialization process. Technical focus areas include climate tech, space, quantum, electro-optics, directed energy, plasma materials, neuroscience devices, medical radiation, medical optics, smart and connected health, and many more.

Tim is a fellow with the Tando Institute and a mentor for Techstars_ Space, the Larta Venture Fellows program, a consultant with the Colorado SBDC TechSource, and an Entrepreneur-in-Residence at the University of Central Florida. He has served four years as an adjunct professor of entrepreneurship at Ringling College of Art + Design.

Among his entrepreneurial endeavors, Tim's art hobby became

a successful venture. As an abstract artist, he tells innovation and brand stories for clients such as IndyCar, Major League Baseball, Budweiser, Tod's of Italy, American Express Centurion Events, and Aston Martin.

Tim's Erdos-Bacon number is 10: Erdos of 7 for being Principal Investigator on "Laser Cladding Modeling and Operation Applied to Plasma-Facing Materials" and Bacon of 3 for his role in "Cuckold Picasso," an award-winning short film.

DEDICATION

This book is dedicated to Anne and Cru. Thank you for all of your love and support.

A heartfelt thank you to all of those who helped to contribute to this book in many different ways. Thank you Anne and Cru for your love and support. Thank you to my peers in "The Syndicate" for all of the commercialization camaraderie - in particular for direct advice on some of the thoughts expressed in the book to Tanya, Earle, Shaun, Ben, Emilie, Lynn and Len. Thank you to my mentor, Jim and also my mental performance coach, Dr. S, who especially encouraged me to write my book.

Thank you to professional editing from Emilie Clemmens, PhD and Lauren Udwari.

Made in United States
Orlando, FL
15 January 2025